Planning Extreme Programming

The XP Series

Kent Beck, Series Advisor

Extreme Programming, familiarly known as XP, is a discipline of business and software development that focuses both parties on common, reachable goals. XP teams produce quality software at a sustainable pace. The practices that make up "book" XP are chosen for their dependence on human creativity and acceptance of human frailty.

Although XP is often presented as a list of practices, XP is not a finish line. You don't get better and better grades at doing XP until you finally receive the coveted gold star. XP is a starting line. It asks the question, 'How little can we do and still build great software?'

The beginning of the answer is that if we want to leave software development uncluttered, we must be prepared to completely embrace the few practices we adopt. Half measures leave problems unsolved to be addressed by further half measures. Eventually you are surrounded by so many half measures that you can no longer see that the heart of the value programmers create comes from programming.

I say, "The beginning of the answer…" because there is no final answer. The authors in the XP Series have been that and done there, and returned to tell their story. The books in this series are the signposts they have planted along the way, "Here lie dragons," "Scenic drive next 15 km," "Slippery when wet."

Excuse me, I gotta go program.

Titles in the Series

Extreme Programming Explained: Embrace Change, Kent Beck
Extreme Programming Installed, Ron Jeffries, Ann Anderson and Chet Hendrickson
Planning Extreme Programming, Kent Beck and Martin Fowler

Planning Extreme Programming

Kent Beck
Martin Fowler

Illustrated by Jennifer Kohnke

ADDISON–WESLEY

Boston • San Francisco • New York • Toronto • Montreal
London • Munich • Paris • Madrid
Capetown • Sydney • Tokyo • Singapore • Mexico City

Many of the designations used by manufacturers and sellers to distinguish their products are claimed as trademarks. Where those designations appear in this book, and we were aware of a trademark claim, the designations have been printed in initial capital letters or in all capitals.

The authors and publisher have taken care in the preparation of this book, but make no expressed or implied warranty of any kind and assume no responsibility for errors or omissions. No liability is assumed for incidental or consequential damages in connection with or arising out of the use of the information or programs contained herein.

The publisher offers discounts on this book when ordered in quantity for special sales. For more information, please contact

Pearson Education Corporate Sales Division
One Lake Street
Upper Saddle River, NJ 07458
(800) 382-3419
corpsales@pearsontechgroup.com

Visit AW on the Web: www.awl.com/cseng/

Library of Congress Cataloging-in-Publication Data
Beck, Kent.
  Planning eXtreme programming / Kent Beck, Martin Fowler.
    p. cm. (The XP series)
  ISBN 0-201-71091-9
   1. Computer software—Development. 2. eXtreme programming. I. Fowler, Martin,
II. Title.

  QA76.76.D47 B4335 2000
  005.3—dc21

00-064306

ISBN 0-201-71091-9

Text printed on recycled paper

1 2 3 4 5 6 7 8 9 10—MA—0403020100
First printing, October 2000

To our Cindies...

Contents

> *We plan to ensure that we are always doing the most important thing left to do, to coordinate effectively with other people, and to respond quickly to unexpected events.*

> *Software development is risky. People involved have many fears of what may go wrong. To develop effectively we must acknowledge these fears.*

> *We use driving as a metaphor for developing software. Driving is not about pointing the car in one direction and holding to it; driving is about making lots of little course corrections.*

> *Our planning process relies on clearly separating the roles of business people and software people. This ensures that business people make all the business decisions and software people make all the technical decisions.*

Foreword

In *On War,* Carl von Clausewitz tells us that military history is a pendulum swinging back and forth between the relative advantages of armor and of mobility. The knights in shining armor were able to dominate any knight without, but they were no match for the quick, nearly naked pony warriors that swept across the plains with Genghis Kahn and his Mongols. Light cavalry itself was doomed as soon as there were tanks, and tanks were no match for fleet-footed Palestinian teenagers with Sagger missiles. With the Maginot Line, the French were gambling that the pendulum had swung again toward armor, but it hadn't, and the Germans simply went around it.

In the field of IT, we are just emerging from a time in which armor (process) has been king. And now we are moving into a time when only mobility matters. Building a product the right way still *sounds* like a laudable goal, but—let's face it—what really matters today is building it *fast*. Because we are process-obsessed in our field, we have tended to react to this new imperative as we reacted to the imperatives thrust upon us in the 1980s and 1990s. We have asked, "What shall we add to our process to deal with this new situation?" No answer to that question is going to be right because the question itself is wrong.

What the new mobility imperative requires is that we *subtract* from process: We need to get light.

"Getting light" means more than just abandoning heavy process and its attendant mountain of documentation. It means investing in people so they can work quickly and effectively without formal process and without generating a ton of paper. No one has a better vision of how this is done than Kent Beck and Martin Fowler.

The XP movement they have founded is a way to make IT projects light and quick. The principles of XP are not just another methodology, another process. They are the antithesis of process. They are means to make process irrelevant.

Because XP projects are completely different, it stands to reason that managing them is different too. *Planning Extreme Programming* focuses on how a team of XP-empowered developers is optimally led. Beck and Fowler's prescriptions are often wry, sometimes wise, and almost always bang on target.

XP is the most important movement in our field today. I predict that it will be as essential to the present generation as the SEI and its Capability Maturity Model were to the last.

Tom DeMarco
Camden, Maine

Preface

This is a book about planning software projects. We are writing it mostly for project managers—those who have to plan and track the correspondence of the planning with reality. We also are writing it for programmers and customers, who have a vital role to play in planning and developing software.

Planning is not about predicting the future. When you make a plan for developing a piece of software, development is not going to go like that. Not ever. Your customers wouldn't even be happy if it did, because by the time the software gets there, the customers don't want what was planned; they want something different.

Like so many, we enjoy Eisenhower's quotation: "In preparing for battle I have always found that plans are useless, but planning is indispensable."[1] That's why this isn't a book about plans; it's about planning. And planning is so valuable and important, so vital, that it deserves to go on a little every day, as long as development lasts.

If you follow the advice in this book, you are going to have a new problem to solve every day—planning—but we won't apologize for that, because without planning, software development inevitably goes off the rails.

The scope of this book is deliberately narrow. It covers how to plan and track software development for XP projects. It's based on our experience

---

1. Richard Nixon, *Six Crises* (New York: Touchstone Press, 1990).

as consultants and coaches, together with the experience of the growing band of early adopters who are using XP.

As a result this isn't a book about the whole of project management. We don't cover typical project manager jobs such as personnel evaluation, recruiting, and budgeting. We don't address the issues of large projects with hordes of developers, nor do we say anything about planning in the context of other software processes, or of planning other activities. We think there are principles and techniques here that everyone can use, but we have stuck to the parts of the process we know—getting everybody on the team pointed in one direction, discovering when this is no longer true, and restoring harmony.

XP (Extreme Programming) is a system of practices (you can use the *m*-word if you want to; we'd rather not, thank you) that a community of software developers is evolving to address the problems of quickly delivering quality software, and then evolving it to meet changing business needs.

XP isn't just about planning. It covers all aspects of small team software development—design, testing, implementation, deployment, and maintenance. However, planning is a key piece of the XP puzzle. (For an overview of XP, read *Extreme Programming Explained: Embrace Change*. While you're at it, buy copies of all of the rest of our books, too.)

XP addresses long projects by breaking them into a sequence of self-contained, one- to three-week mini-projects. During each iteration

- ✧ Customers pick the features to be added.
- ✧ Programmers add the features so they are completely ready to be deployed.
- ✧ Programmers and customers write and maintain automated tests to demonstrate the presence of these features.
- ✧ Programmers evolve the design of the system to gracefully support all the features in the system.

Without careful planning, the process falls apart.

- ✧ The team must choose the best possible features to implement.
- ✧ The team must react as positively as possible to the inevitable setbacks.
- ✧ Team members must not overcommit, or they will slow down.

- The team must not undercommit, or customers won't get value for their money.
- Team members must figure out clearly where they are and report this accurately, so that everyone can adjust their plans accordingly

The job of the daily planner is to help keep the team on track in all these areas.

We come by our project planning ideas by necessity. As consultants, we are usually introduced to projects when they are mostly dead. The projects typically aren't doing any planning, or they are drowning in too much planning of the wrong sort.

The resulting ideas are the simplest planning ideas we could think of that could possibly work. But above all, remember all the planning techniques in the world, including these, can't save you if you forget that software is built by human beings. In the end keep the human beings focused, happy, and motiviated and they will deliver.

Kent Beck, Merlin, Oregon
Martin Fowler, Melrose, Massachusetts http://www.martinfowler.com
July 2000

I have a cunning plan.
—*Baldrick,* Blackadder

Acknowledgments

Thanks to our reviewers: Mark Windholtz, Ralph Johnson, Uncle Bob Martin, John Brewer, Phil Goodwin, Jean-Marc Heneman, Erik Meade, Alan Francis, Josu Oyanguren, Jim Stearns, Joel Jones, Bill Caputo, Randy Coulman, Andrew Nielsen, Brian Button, Don Wells, Gary Clayburg, James Goebel, Paul Sinnett, Bill deHora, Andreas Stankewitz, Frank Westphal, Georg Tuparev, Stuart Donovan, Joi Ellis, Alistair Cockburn, Matt Simons, Rob Mee, and Joshua Kerievsky.

Kent would like to thank Cindee, Bethany, Lincoln, Lindsey, Forrest, and Joëlle for their gift of time. Also, watching my brilliant coauthor Martin learn to skip rocks was the purest joy I've had in a good long time.

Martin would like to thank the folks at ThoughtWorks for trying and pushing beyond many of these ideas and for giving him the time to write this. But especially to thank Cindy for more reasons than would fit in this book.

Together, we'd like to thank our editor, Mike Hendrickson, and the staff at AWL: Heather Peterson, Heather Olszyk, Mike Guzikowski, and Tyrrell Albaugh.

Thanks to Bob Coe and Ron Jeffries for trusting us, then going beyond.

Our deepest thanks go to Robert Cecil "Uncle Bob" Martin. You'll find many of his words and thoughts in these pages.

Chapter 1

Why Plan?

The best-laid schemes o' mice an' men
Gang aft a gley.
—Robert Burns, "To a Mouse"

We plan to ensure that we are always doing the most important thing left to do, to coordinate effectively with other people, and to respond quickly to unexpected events.

When Kent was about ten, he went fly-fishing for the first time in the Idaho panhandle. After a fruitless, sweaty day in pursuit of brook trout, he and his friends headed for home. After half an hour of stumbling through dense trees, they realized they were lost. Kent started to panic—fast breathing, tunnel vision, chills. Then someone suggested a plan—they would walk uphill until they hit a logging road they knew was up there. Instantly, the panic disappeared.

Kent was struck at the time by the importance of having a plan. Without the plan, he was going to do something stupid, or just go catatonic. With the plan he was calm again.

Plans in software development work the same way. If you know you have a tight deadline, but you make a plan and the plan says you can make the deadline, then you'll start on your first task with a sense of urgency but still working as well as possible. After all, you have enough time. This is exactly the behavior that is most likely to cause the plan to come true. Panic leads to fatigue, defects, and communication breakdowns.

But we've also seen plans lead to trouble. They can be a huge time sink, dragging days out of people who'd rather be doing something productive. Plans can be used as a stick to beat people with, and worst of all, they can conceal trouble until it's too late to deal with it.

Why We Should Plan

We don't plan so we can predict the future. Business and software are changing too rapidly for prediction to be possible. Even if it were possible to predict what we needed in three years, it wouldn't necessarily help because between now and then we need so many different things.

The more obvious it is that you should do something, the more important it is to ask why. You must do some planning when tackling a serious software development project. Therefore, before you start planning a project, you have to understand why you need to carry out the project. Without understanding why you need the project, how will you be able to tell if you have succeeded?

We plan because

✧ We need to ensure that we are always working on the most important thing we need to do.

✧ We need to coordinate with other people.

✧ When unexpected events occur we need to understand the consequences for the first two.

The first is the obvious reason for planning. There's nothing more frustrating than working hard on a part of the system only to find that it doesn't really matter and gets scrapped in the next release of the system. Time spent doing one thing is time not spent doing something else, and if that something else is important then we may fail.

Say it's two o'clock and we're in Boston. We want to drive up to Acadia, but we'd also like to get haircuts and hit Freeport for camping gear. Last time we drove up to Acadia it took us five hours with no stops. So we see some options. If we shoot straight up to Acadia we can be there by seven o'clock. If we want to stop for dinner on the way, say an hour, we will be there by eight. To get haircuts we'd need another hour, so that would be nine. Visiting Freeport would add another hour. We look at what's most important to us. If we want to be fed, equipped, not too late, and we could care less about our appearance, we might decide to drop the haircut. A plan helps us see our options.

Coordination is why everyone else wants us to plan. We get a call from our wives to meet for dinner in Bar Harbor. Since it's two o'clock we know we can meet them if we drive right up, stop in Freeport, and be there around eight. Software is full of such coordination: marketing announcements, financial periods, or management promises. Planning allows us to get an idea of what is reasonable.

But planning is only as good as the estimates that the plans are based on, and estimates always come second to actuals. If we hit a horrible traffic jam, all the planning in the world can't help us make that dinner date. The real world has this horrible habit of destroying plans, as Mr. Burns noted in this chapter's opening quote.

Planning still helps when the real world intrudes because it allows us to consider the effects of the unexpected event. Leaving at two o'clock, we hit bad traffic and don't get to Portland until five. We know we usually get there after an hour and a half, so our experience (and plan) tells us to call our friends to put dinner back to half past eight and drop the visit to Freeport. Planning allows us both to adjust what we do and to coordinate with others. The key is to adjust the plan as soon as we know the effect of the event. Our wives would much rather know about our delay at five than at eight, and it would be really annoying to spend time in Freeport and only later realize that we've really screwed up dinner with our Cindies. (We don't even want to contemplate the consequences of that; in comparison, software failures are minor events.)

What We Need in Planning

Planning is something that people do at various scales. You might plan your day's activities. The team plans out its tasks for a couple of weeks. Development and business lay out a plan for the next year. Senior managers develop plans for a large organization. If you are driving from Boston to Acadia, you won't plan every curve in the road, but you will want to figure out which roads to take and when to change from one to another. You're not going to expect to arrive to the minute, but we know there is some limit of lateness that requires the apologetic phone call.

In order to carry out the coordination it's vital to have an accurate picture of how far you are along in the plan. On a road trip this is fairly straightforward. You can measure mileage, take into account the nature of the roads, and come up with a rough schedule with significant points along the way. If you are very late arriving at Portland, you can easily tell, and thus estimate, the delay in reaching Bar Harbor. Software's virtual nature again conspires against this property. With all the degrees of freedom it can be very difficult to find out whether you are 70 percent done or 30 percent done. It's like taking a road trip where you don't know whether you've gone 30 miles or 300 miles. Without any frame of reference you feel uncomfortable. If your dinner date doesn't know how close you are and it's getting late, she is uncomfortable, too.

Any software planning technique must try to create visibility, so everyone involved in the project can really see how far along a project is. This means that you need clear milestones, ones that cannot be fudged, and clearly represent progress. Milestones must also be things that everyone involved in the project, including the customer, can understand and learn to trust.

Plans are about figuring out a likely course of events and the consequences of the inevitable changes. We need different plans at different scales. Yet plans must also be both simple to build and simple to keep up-to-date. Large and complex plans are not helpful because they cost too much to build and maintain. Since plans involve coordination, they must be comprehensible to everyone who is affected by the plan— another reason for simplicity.

Plans must be honest, including all the information you have to date. Plans should make it difficult for anyone to be fooled by reports of progress unrelated to reality.

The Planning Trap

It's the preceding paragraph that gives us a hint as to why planning can be a trap. This is because there is another reason why people plan: to demonstrate they are in control of events

But controlling events is an oxymoron: You can't control events; you can only control your reactions. Even then the amount of control you have is limited. Events change plans. Once you hit that traffic jam, either dinner or Freeport is affected. You can't just carry on with the plan and pretend everything is okay. That would be stupid.

Yet we've seen this happen plenty of times. If things don't go according to plan, then the planner is afraid he will be blamed. That fear induces the planner to say that the plan is still on track. The planner might admit to himself that the plan is off track, but if the plan is complicated enough the planner can even hide that. Nothing is more important than to say to the outside world that everything is still going according to plan.

The plan is diverging from reality, turning into an illusion. Worse, the planner spends energy trying to maintain the illusion. Developers gradually lose motivation. If the plan's an illusion, why try to follow it?

Perhaps the project will sort itself out in the end. Occasionally it does. Perhaps someone else has even worse problems. More often the gap between illusion and reality grows until the illusion is unsustainable. Things get ugly. The customer is angry because she has made her own plans based on the illusion, made promises that she can't keep. The programmers are angry because they've worked hard, done their best, but now they are being shouted at for not doing the impossible and making the illusion real.

Events happen. Plans change. If things seems to be going exactly according to plan, that's usually a sign of trouble. The worst thing that can happen to a project is the divergence between the plan and reality. So don't fall into that trap. Keep your plans honest, and expect them to always change.

Chapter 2

Fear

Courage! What makes a King out of a slave?
Courage! What makes the flag on the mast to wave?
Courage! What makes the elephant charge his tusk, in the misty mist or the dusky dusk?
What makes the muskrat guard his musk?
Courage! What makes the sphinx the seventh wonder?
Courage! What makes the dawn come up like thunder?
Courage! What makes the Hottentot so hot? What puts the "ape" in apricot?
What have they got that I ain't got?
—Cowardly Lion, The Wizard of OZ

Software development is risky. People involved have many fears
of what may go wrong. To develop effectively we must
acknowledge these fears.

Why do we need a software process? For the same reason that we need laws, governments, and taxes: fear.

The Declaration of Independence says:

That among these [rights] are life, liberty, and the pursuit of happiness.
That to secure these rights, governments are instituted among men,
deriving their just powers from the consent of the governed.

Though the profundity of these words may distract us, consider the word *secure.* We institute governments because we are afraid of losing our rights.

By the same token, we institute software processes because we are afraid. Customers are afraid that

- They won't get what they asked for.
- They'll ask for the wrong thing.
- They'll pay too much for too little.
- They must surrender control of their career to techies who don't care.
- They won't ever see a meaningful plan.
- The plans they do see will be fairy tales.
- They won't know what's going on.
- They'll be held to their first decisions and won't be able to react to changes in the business.
- No one will tell them the truth.

Developers are afraid, too. They fear that

- They will be told to do more than they know how to do.
- They will be told to do things that don't make sense.
- They are too stupid.
- They are falling behind technically.
- They will be given responsibility without authority.
- They won't be given clear definitions of what needs to be done.
- They'll have to sacrifice quality for deadlines.
- They'll have to solve hard problems without help.
- They won't have enough time to succeed.

Unacknowledged Fear Is the Source of All Software Project Failures

If these fears are not put on the table and dealt with, then developers and customer each try to protect themselves by building walls. They refuse to share critical information:

"If I tell the engineers about this, they'll spend months trying to figure it out instead of doing what I need."

"If I tell the customer how quickly I got this done, he'll expect me to do everything that fast."

They exaggerate, tell half-truths, lie, cover up, and work at cross-purposes. They build huge, useless political and procedural structures aimed at protection instead of success.

In order to be successful, a development process must be instituted among customers and developers that secures certain inalienable rights.

Customer Bill of Rights

- ✧ You have the right to an overall plan, to know what can be accomplished when and at what cost.
- ✧ You have the right to get the most possible value out of every programming week.
- ✧ You have the right to see progress in a running system, proven to work by passing repeatable tests that you specify.
- ✧ You have the right to change your mind, to substitute functionality, and to change priorities without paying exorbitant costs.
- ✧ You have the right to be informed of schedule changes, in time to choose how to reduce the scope to restore the original date. You can cancel at any time and be left with a useful working system reflecting investment to date.

Programmer Bill of Rights

- ✧ You have the right to know what is needed, with clear declarations of priority.
- ✧ You have the right to produce quality work at all times.
- ✧ You have the right to ask for and receive help from peers, managers, and customers.
- ✧ You have the right to make and update your own estimates.
- ✧ You have the right to accept your responsibilities instead of having them assigned to you.

If we are going to develop well, we must create a culture that makes it possible for programmers and customers to acknowledge their fears and accept their rights and responsibilities. Without such guarantees, we cannot be courageous. We huddle in fear behind fortress walls, building them ever stronger, adding ever more weight to the development processes we have adopted. We continually add cannonades and battlements, documents and reviews, procedures and sign-offs, moats with crocodiles, torture chambers, and huge pots of boiling oil.

But when our fears are acknowledged and our rights are accepted, then we can be courageous. We can set goals that are hard to reach and collaborate to make those goals. We can tear down the structures that we built out of fear and that impede us. We will have the courage to do only what is necessary and no more, to spend our time on what's important rather than on protecting ourselves.

Chapter 3

Driving Software

Of course I'm an excellent driver.
—Raymond, Rain Man

We use driving as a metaphor for developing software. Driving is not about pointing the car in one direction and holding to it; driving is about making lots of little course corrections.

The driving story featured prominently in *Extreme Programming Explained*, but it is central to XP so we repeat it here. If you read *XPE*, you'll want to read this chapter only to see if we've somehow managed to make the story a bit more dramatic.

It was a beautiful sunny day. Kent and his mom were driving along a straight stretch of I-5 near Chico. He was about 12 years old.

"It's about time you learn how to drive," said Mom.

"Really?" Excitement bubbled in Kent's chest.

"Yes. Now, what I want you to do is get the car right in between the lines and pointed absolutely straight," said Mom.

"I can do that."

Kent very carefully lines up the star on the beige Mercedes 240D dead straight to the horizon. His eyebrows raise a little at just how easy this driving thing really is. After a moment, his eyes drift to a roadside sign.

gggggrrrrrrccccchhhh (hey, you try to write down a sound that combines wheels on gravel with a preadolescent yelp). Kent's mouth goes dry; his heart pounds.

"Okay," says Mom, concealing a smile, "that's not how you drive a car. Driving a car is not about getting the car pointed in the right direction. Driving a car is about constantly making little corrections. You drift a little this way, you steer a little that way. This way, that way, as long as you are driving."

You don't drive software development by getting your project pointed in the right direction (The Plan). You drive software development by seeing that you are drifting a little this way and steering a little that way. This way, that way, as long as you develop the software.

One very vocal opponent of XP once used the phrase: "Ready . . . Fire . . . Aim!" The intent was clearly pejorative. How can you hit a target unless you aim first? The point, however, is that we are not trying to hit a target. Instead, we are trying to maximize the benefit of a process.

The driving metaphor helps us once again. Your first act as you get into the car is not turning the wheel so that it points toward your destination. Your first act is usually to turn on the ignition. Indeed, the initial direction of motion has little to do with your destination and much more to do with your local circumstances. You might want to back out of your garage before heading for Peoria. Though you probably have a destination in mind and a route planned, that route and destination are always subject to change. The radio may warn you of heavy traffic, causing you to change your route. Your spouse may call on the cell phone and ask you to pick up some milk, causing you to modify your destination.

Software development is a process. It can go well, or it can go badly. To keep it going well we must continually direct it. To direct it we must frequently assess the direction it is going, compare this to the direction we want it to go, and then make careful adjustments. Thus, good project management can be characterized by: "Ready . . . Fire . . . Aim . . . Aim . . . Aim . . . Aim . . . Aim . . ."

Chapter 4

Balancing Power

Our planning process relies on clearly separating the roles of business people and software people. This ensures that business people make all the business decisions and software people make all the technical decisions.

The key to project management is balancing power between the business people and the programmers. Done right, software project management has

✧ Business people making business decisions
✧ Technical people making technical decisions

Isn't this just like saying that Wensleydale is the Queen of Cheeses? Of course business people make business decisions.

What about this one?

"We think this system will take six months to develop."

"You have three months."

"What can we take out?"

"Nothing. Everything has to be there."

Guessing how long something is likely to take to program is a purely technical decision. The programmers pool their experience on similar projects, stir their understanding of how the new system is different, and pick a number off a dartboard. No, actually it's a little more systematic than that (see Chapter 12). However, tough as estimating is, the programmers are in a much better position to guess than anyone else. So estimating is a technical decision.

In the dialog above, taken from an actual doomed project, estimating was done by a business person for business reasons. The resulting estimate, that the work in question would take three months, cannot possibly have been better than the programmers' estimate of six months. However, without intervention, everyone went on to the next stage of planning based on grossly inaccurate information. The resulting plan, no matter how cheap, flexible, and communicable, was, simply put, tripe.

If business people occasionally make technical decisions, at least technical people don't make business decisions.

Uh, how about this one?

"I have ten things to do. I know I'll only get five of them done. I'll work on this DCOM/CORBA infrastructure first. It looks cool."

Stop. Choosing the relative priority between features is a business decision. Whether another user interface feature is more important than another report column is a business decision. The business people take what they know of the market, combine it with their experience of similar systems, then pick a feature off a dartboard. No, actually it can be a little more systematic than that (sometimes it is; sometimes it isn't). Tough as it is to guess which feature to do next, the business folks are in a much better position than are the programmers to make this decision.

Business decisions in planning are

- ✧ Dates
- ✧ Scope
- ✧ Priority

Technical decisions in planning are

- ✧ Estimates

If we have the right people making the decisions, planning will go as well as possible. We'll be able to deal with our disasters. We'll do it by reducing the number of disasters as much as possible, by finding out about the disasters as quickly as possible, and by maintaining as many options as possible for as long as possible.

Balancing political power may seem like a tall order for a simple project manager. If the world can't do it between nations after a couple of millennia of concerted effort, what chance do you have?

Balancing power is not as tough as it sounds. Create a simple set of rules that tend to cause the technical people to make the technical decisions and the business people to make the business decisions.

The Customer

In XP we talk a lot about the customer. By *customer* we mean the person who makes the business decisions. Often you don't have a single literal customer. You have users, business management, operations, all sorts of people who are customers. If you do shrink-wrap software you may have thousands of customers. However, for XP to work, the customer must speak with one voice. Some people call such an animal a product manager or a requirements champion. We use the term *customer* because that's who this person represents.

A lot of planning processes see the customer as some kind of disembodied entity outside of software development who provides requirements. You interpret, tease, do JAD sessions—but the customer is outside the team.

XP is not like that. XP planning assumes that the customer is very much part of the team, even if the customer works for a different company and the rest of the team works for a contractor. The customer must be part of the team because his role is far too important to leave to an outsider. Any (XP) project will fail if the customer isn't able to steer.

So the customer's job is a huge responsibility. All the best talent and technology and process in the world will fail when the customer isn't up to scratch. Sadly, it's also a role on which we can't offer particularly sage advice. After all, we're nerds, not business people. But here's what we know for sure.

Finding a Customer

Because the customer is such a critical role, it's important to find someone who will play it well. A good customer

- ✦ Understands the domain well by working in that domain, and also by understanding how it works (not always the same thing)
- ✦ Can understand, with development's help, how software can provide business value in the domain
- ✦ Is determined to deliver value regularly and is not afraid to deliver too little rather than nothing
- ✦ Can make decisions about what's needed now and what's needed later
- ✦ Is willing to accept ultimate responsibility for the success or failure of the project

Accepting responsibility for the success or failure of the project seems to be the most difficult part of the role. There is a certain comfort for the customer in maintaining a distance from the team. Behind three feet of requirements documents is about right. In XP this won't work. If you get lost driving, it isn't the car's fault, it's the driver's.

The trickiest thing about XP for a customer is getting used to the rhythm of regular delivery. A lot of processes ask the customer for everything they want. Instead, the customer asks for, and the team delivers, as little as possible—just enough to provide value. There's an argument that says if you can't find a customer who wants to work that way you shouldn't try XP at all.

Guiding the Customer

If you're a customer reading this, then here are some important things to remember.

Ask yourself at all times, "What is the most valuable functionality to have next?" Long-term planning can be fun, but it's regular, little deliveries that keep the money coming in.

Trust the developers' estimates, yet remember they're only estimates and they will get it wrong. Estimating software development is hard; they're doing the best they can and they will get better.

Never let a date slip. Slipping dates is one of the worst habits in software development. You slip just one or two and after a while you're addicted. It isn't completely against the rules to slip a date, it's just that the XP methodology requires you to chop one of your own fingers off each time you do it.

Provide a little valuable functionality every single release, and release to real customers as often as you can. Don't be afraid to release something that's not enough yet. Use your creativity to look for ways that you can take a large new capability and break it up into little pieces so you can keep delivering. If you release frequently enough, you won't have long to wait before you get more of what you want.

Chapter 5

Overviews

The XP process has releases that take a few months, that divide into two-week iterations, that divide into tasks that take a few days. Planning allocates stories (chunks of function) to releases and iterations in reaction to the realities of development.

We're going to outline XP in two ways. If you like an overall understanding before going into details, read the following section first. If you like to go from smaller to larger scale, read the second section of this chapter first.

Top Down

Plant in the spring; harvest in the fall. The world works on cycles. Software development is no different. The planning challenge is that there are two cycles that we need to accommodate and synchronize— the business cycle and the development cycle.

The business cycle revolves around the activities of business:

⬦ Press releases
⬦ Software release, manufacturing, and installation
⬦ Training
⬦ Billing

In the old days this cycle was a leisurely two to three years long. Recently, the cycle has tightened enormously, driven by widespread telecommunications and technical advances in the delivery of software.

Still, the business cycle is at least months long. We will call one of these one- to six-month turns of the business crank a **release**.

The development cycle has always been shorter than the business cycle. The intent of having a shorter cycle was to correct projects in midcourse. Sometimes the interim deliverables documented certain kinds of decisions, as in the requirements, analysis, and design documents of a waterfall. Sometimes they were partly functional systems or subsystems, as in incremental development.

The contraction of the business cycle requires a similar contraction of the development cycle. If we release every few months, then if we want to be able to make midcourse corrections we must shrink the development cycle to no more than a few weeks. We will call one of these one- to three-week development cycles an **iteration**.

The problem with a cycle of a few weeks is that it is impossible to complete anything in a few weeks. You can't complete the analysis, or build the infrastructure, or set up the framework. We have to use some other measure of progress. Since the customers are paying for the software, we'll use a measure they understand—the **story**. A story represents a feature customers want in the software, a story they would like to be able to tell their friends about this great system they are using.

For a few stories to fit into an iteration, the stories have to be fairly small. A story should take a programmer a few days to a few weeks to implement.

What is the result of an iteration? Any activity that comes between finishing the engineering of a release and delivering it to customers represents a risk. We hate risk. So the result of an iteration must be a fully tested, production-ready system.

This may sound impossible. But the first time you go through an iteration, the number of stories is small. If a system is small enough you can test and verify it during the iteration. If you invest in making the verification automatic, when you finish the second iteration the incremental cost of verifying both sets of stories is again small. If you never "get behind on your payments," if the result of each iteration is ready to be used, then the cost of maintaining readiness remains reasonable.

Bottom Up

What if we shrunk the whole software development life cycle to microscopic size, say two weeks? We would still have to solve all the problems we had to solve before—specification, design, implementation, testing, integration, deployment, training, documentation—but now they would be small problems, not big problems, and some of them might disappear entirely.

The various development activities won't be phases inside our little two-week project (let's call it an iteration, just to be conventional). We will have to do a little of each of them every day.

Each iteration contains all the elements of full-scale development. At the end we have shippable software, ready to deploy. It just doesn't contain many features. Maybe it will contain only one feature. So we will have to do another iteration and another and another (hence the name, we suppose). Each iteration will contain a few more features.

One more thing and the picture is complete. One of the purposes of planning is to ensure we always work on the most valuable thing possible at any given time. We can't pick features at random and expect them to be most valuable. We have to begin development by taking a quick look at everything that might be valuable, putting all our cards on the table. At the beginning of each iteration the business (remember the balance of power) will pick the most valuable features for the next iteration.

Now we have a process where planning can do its proper job. The process makes sure we get off to as good a start as possible by laying out the whole of development. The process mitigates requirements risk by picking new requirements every few weeks. The process mitigates implementation risk by breaking planning up into small enough pieces that when one piece blows up it will affect the overall plan as quickly and visibly as possible.

Chapter 6

Too Much to Do

When you are overloaded, don't think of it as not having enough time; think of it as having too much to do. You can't give yourself more time, but you can give yourself less to do, at least for the moment.

We were on a project together once that the team had rescued from impending oblivion. Toward the first release there came a time when it was clear to everyone that we weren't going to make the release date. One day we had a stand-up meeting to discuss the problem. We went around the circle answering the question "What is preventing us from going into production?"

"I don't have enough time."

"I don't have enough time."

"I don't have enough time."

Nobody had enough time. But there was no obvious answer. Everybody went home.

Over Korean food that night (we always ate Korean; it seems to be good for the brain), we were talking about the meeting. Suddenly a cosmic ray collided with a piece of kimchee and we saw the real problem.

The next morning we called another stand-up.

"Repeat after me—I have too much to do."

Shrugs all around, but what the heck.

"I have too much to do."

"I have too much to do."

"I have too much to do."

And so on around the circle until we got to Richard.

"I have too much to do. What is your point?"

The point is that when you don't have enough time you are out of luck. You can't make more time. Not having enough time is a position of hopelessness. And hopelessness breeds frustration, mistakes, burn-out, and failure.

Having too much to do, however, is a situation we all know. When you have too much to do you can

 ✧ Prioritize and not do some things
 ✧ Reduce the size of some of the things you do
 ✧ Ask someone else to do some things

Having too much to do breeds hope. We may not like being there, but at least we know what to do.

Chapter 7

Four Variables

We use four variables to help us think about how to control a project: cost, quality, time, and scope. They are interrelated but affect each other in strange ways.

We've all heard statements like "Cost, time, quality: pick any two." Plenty of people have ways in which they talk about how there are these variables involved in getting something done, and that you can't control them all at once. In planning software projects, we had to add a variable before we could bring our projects under control:

 ⬧ Cost
 ⬧ Quality
 ⬧ Time
 ⬧ Scope

We like to think of them as four levers on some big Victorian steam machine. The four levers control the machine (our project). If you move any lever the others move. You can lock any lever you like, but if you lock three levers you cannot move the fourth.

The catch, however, is that the effect of moving a lever is both delayed and nonlinear. You can't just double the cost, hold everything else the same, and halve the time. So each lever gets its own little instruction manual. (The good news is that the manual wasn't written by a second-rate Victorian novelist.)

Cost

The cost lever is actually several mostly independent levers. Moving any of them can increase or reduce your costs, but each lever has a different effect on the three other primary levers.

The most powerful lever is people. You increase this lever by putting more people on the project. This lever, however, suffers from having both a nonlinear effect and a long delay.

The nonlinearity comes from the communication overhead of having more people. Doubling your team doesn't make you go twice as fast because it increases the amount of communication that needs to go on. There isn't really much guidance we can give you on this, partly because there isn't the data and partly because so many other factors have an effect. All you can do is add some people and measure the effect.

The trouble is you'll have to wait to really see the effect, since adding people causes several changes that take time to play out. The immediate effect is the alarming sight of nothing changing, or even worse, a slowing down. When a new person joins a running team he will initially be of little value because he doesn't know the system or the team. Indeed, he can slow things down because he drains time from other people as they teach him about these things. The more people you add, the bigger this slowdown effect is. Add enough people and the project can come to a big crunching halt. This is the origin for Brooks' Law, "Adding people to a late project just makes it later."[1]

There are other ways to spend money. Spending on tools can be like adding people. But you will slow down as people learn how to use the tools, and only when they become comfortable with the tools will you know whether they will help.

Spending some money can have a very good return: faster computers, bigger monitors. Don't be afraid to spend money to keep motivation up. Well- motivated developers are much more effective than people whose motivation sags.

---

1. Frederick P. Brooks, Jr., *The Mythical Man-Month: Essays on Software Engineering*, (Reading, MA: Addison-Wesley, 1995).

Overtime doesn't help. Although in the very short term it does speed up the team, if you do it for any length of time you will get bitten badly. The big killer is motivation. It's much better to have a motivated programmer work seven hours than a tired, distracted programmer work ten. Even if the programmers want to work long hours it's not a good idea. Long hours make people tired, tired people make mistakes, and mistakes take time to fix. We've both gone into clients in the morning and spent all day chasing a bug that was put in at ten o'clock the previous night. Particularly with young Silicon Valley teams, where long hours are such an important tribal ritual, we have to work hard to get people not to do overtime. If they really have no life, get them to play computer games in the evening instead. It's much more productive to have castles mown down by trebuchets than it is to slip bugs into complicated software.

Quality

Quality is really two levers: external and internal quality. External quality is the quality perceived by the customer. This includes bugs but may also include nonfunctional requirements such as how the GUI looks and how fast the software is.

Try to move nonfunctional requirements over to scope. Make a story for something like "Make the user interface more pleasing" or "Get average claim processing time to under 300 ms." As we'll see later, scope is the best lever to operate.

Bugs are often also a scoping issue. Often you may have to trade defects for stories. We'll talk about this more in Chapter 22.

The other lever is internal quality. This reflects the quality of the internals of the system: how well it is designed, how good the internal tests are, and so on. This is a very dangerous lever to play with. If you allow internal quality to drop you'll get a small immediate increase in speed, rapidly followed by a much bigger decrease in speed. As a result you must keep an eagle eye on this lever and make sure it is always up as far as it can go. Nothing kills speed more effectively than poor internal quality. That's why Extreme Programming puts so much attention on practices like testing and refactoring. If you keep internal quality high you can see where you are and predict where you can go.

Time and Scope

So the first two levers are difficult to work with at best, and certainly impossible for exerting any short-term control. Time and scope are left as the best levers to operate. With most of our planning, we assume that qualtity and cost are fixed.

The question is how do we best operate the time and scope levers?

The complicated thing about these two levers is that they are placed on very different parts of the machine. The scope lever is right in front of you and just loves to be pushed up. Every time you pass the machine you want to push that lever up a bit and add another little story to the project. The machine responds with a cute little gurgle as an instant reward. "Yes, sir, we can do that, too, sir."

The time lever, however, is really awkwardly placed. You have to crawl on your hands and knees, crane your neck, and flip open the door labeled "Beware of the leopard." Because the effects on time when adding scope are so hard to see, people don't usually realize what's happening until it's too late and the machine is out of control.

Planning must make the time lever visible, so that every time you add scope you can immediately see the effects on time. You just need to arrange the mirrors to avoid the smoke.

You only really know where you are when you are at the end of project. So you need to end the project every few weeks—that's why we use iterations. The iterations force us to look at the time lever every few weeks so we can't avoid seeing the consequences of changing scope.

Planning now becomes a matter of figuring out which stories to build in each iteration.

We need a planning style that

- ✧ Preserves the programmers' confidence that the plan is possible
- ✧ Preserves the customers' confidence that they are getting as much as they can
- ✧ Costs as little to execute as possible (because we'll be planning often, but nobody pays for plans; they pay for results)

At this point we are getting tired of our Victorian machine and feel another analogy coming on.

Shopping for Stories

What if planning for a piece of software was like shopping? When you go grocery shopping for the week, you have a budget. You go into the store and look around at the items and their prices, and you think about what you need to accomplish. If you are feeding a horde of teen-agers, you tend toward rice and beans. If the boss if coming over for dinner, you get steak for one night and go easy the rest of the week.

The elements of the analogy are

- ✧ The items
- ✧ The prices
- ✧ The budget
- ✧ The constraints

Applying the analogy to planning:

- ✧ Items are the stories.
- ✧ Prices are the estimates on each story.
- ✧ Budget is the team's measured progress in terms of these estimates.
- ✧ Constraints are the business and technology constraints as they are discovered by the customer and the team.

The shopping analogy can carry us a little further.

- ✧ *Sales*—If reports turn out to be easier to implement than expected, that's having a sale on reports. "Attention software shoppers. Reports are going two for one on aisle 14."
- ✧ *Rain check*—If you have to discard a new wizard in the middle of a release to save the end date, that's taking a rain check. "IOU one wizard."
- ✧ *Inflation*—If graphics are harder to add than expected, the prices go up. "Due to circumstances beyond our control, graphics are now $1.49 per pound."

Any time we have to decide what to do, we will go shopping. Who chooses how big the items are and who sets the prices will all vary, but the strategy is the same. We will shop for $5 million worth of software and we will shop for next week's tasks.

Chapter 8

Yesterday's Weather

You can't put ten pounds of shit in a five-pound bag.
—Anyone who has tried

As the basis for your planning, assume you'll do as much this
week as you did last week.

How big is the bag? This shopping metaphor is all well and good, but what is the budget? How much do you commit to doing in the next *n* months?

If you commit to too much, development proceeds under a cloud. The programmers know they are doomed. They don't do their best work. They don't communicate clearly. The political sophisticates play Schedule Chicken, where the first person to point out the impossibility of the task ahead is labeled a loser, not a "team player."

Okay, we don't want to do that. Neither do we want to undercommit. If it turns out we can go twice as fast as we thought we could, the business will take a while to catch up. The press releases won't mention half of the cool new features. Sales won't understand what all is in the product. And it is a matter of pride for programmers to put out 100 percent.

How can we navigate such an emotional and business minefield? How can we come up with a complicated rule-making apparatus that accurately captures and balances all the technical and emotional information that is available?

We don't—surprise, surprise. Instead we opt for a simple rule that works pretty well in most circumstances:

Say you'll do as much tomorrow as you actually got done today.

The Story

Here is an apocryphal story. Some country's weather service (not yours, but perhaps ours) spent a bazillion dollars on a sophisticated new weather prediction system. Lights flashed, cards spewed, tapes spun, and out came predictions that were about 70 percent accurate. The people who authorized spending the bazillion dollars were quite impressed.

Then one day someone noticed a simpler way to get the same accuracy. Every day predict that tomorrow's weather will be exactly the same as today's.

That's why we call our rule Yesterday's Weather.

How It Works

Assume for the moment that each feature you are going to implement takes the same amount of effort (see Chapter 12 for what we really do). If we did five features last month and we're asked how much we can do this month, we say "five." If we have gotten three features done every two weeks for a while and we're asked how much we can do in the next six months, we say "3 features/iteration × 2 iterations/month × 6 months = 36 features."

Here are some of the emergent properties of this rule:

- ✧ We won't habitually overestimate our abilities. We have to use actual accomplishment. If we overestimate once, we won't be able to the next time.
- ✧ If we are overcommitted, we will tend to try to finish some items in any given time period instead of half finishing them all. It is *so* embarrassing to tell the customer they can have zero features next time.
- ✧ On the other hand, if we have a disastrous period, we are guaranteed a little breathing space to recover.
- ✧ Everyone learns to trust our numbers because they are so easy to explain.
- ✧ Our estimates automatically track all kinds of changes—changes to the team, new technology, dramatic changes in product direction.

Chapter 9

Scoping a Project

To get a quick feel for how big the project is, run the planning process at coarse resolution.

Let's say you're the only one on the project so far. What's the first step? How can you use shopping to bring a project into existence?

- *Items*—Big stories
- *Prices*—Rough estimates of the time to implement each story
- *Budget*—Roughly how many people you have to work on the project
- *Constraints*—Supplied by someone with business knowledge

The purpose of this first plan is to quickly answer the question "Does the project make any sense at all?" Often these sanity plans are made before there are any technical people on the project at all. Don't worry about getting perfect numbers. If the project makes any sense then you'll invest enough to prepare a plan you have some confidence in.

What if we were to implement a space-age travel system? (For the full story of the system see Example of Stories on page 53.) We might have a few big stories in mind. Before we can assign prices to them, we have to know a little more about the system. We ask a few questions:

◇ How many reservations do we need to handle?

◇ How much of the time do we need to have the system available?

◇ What kind of machines will be used to access the system?

With that in mind, we can guess at how long a team of ten would need to implement each feature as shown in Table 9.1.

TABLE 9.1 Stories

Story	Estimate
Book a space flight	2 months
Book a hotel	1 month
Check itinerary	1 month
Adventure trips	2 months
Holographic planetary simulation	6 months
Cross-species orientation	4 months
Auto-translator	8 months

We make some simplifying assumptions as we go along.

◇ The stories are completely independent of each other.

◇ We will develop the necessary infrastructure along with the story, but only the infrastructure absolutely needed for that story.

We know these assumptions aren't exactly accurate, but then again neither is anything else. If we were trying to predict the future, this would worry us. Since we aren't, it doesn't.

So, the bottom line is that we can implement the system in 24 months.

The shouting starts. "We have to go to market in six months, tops, or we're dead." Yes, we understand. "If you can't do it, we'll hire someone who can." You should do that, but perhaps we can talk a little first. "You programmers can't tell me what to do." Of course not, but perhaps you would like to know what you can't do.

Now the negotiation starts. "What if we just made a booking system first? We'd need the first three stories. That's four months. But we can't launch without the holographic simulation. What can you give me in two months?"

Within a few hours or days, we have a rough plan from which we can move forward.

Making the Big Plan

The purpose of the big plan is to answer the question "Should we invest more?" We address this question in three ways:

- Break the problem into pieces.
- Bring the pieces into focus by estimating them.
- Defer less valuable pieces.

Start with a conversation about the system (this works best if you involve at least one other person). As you talk, write down your thoughts, one per index card. If your thoughts get too detailed, stop writing until you get abstract again.

Some cards will contain business functionality. These are stories. Lay these out in the middle of a big table. Some of the cards will contain ideas that are context—throughput, reliability, budget, sketches of happy customers. Set these to one side.

Now you need to estimate how long each story would take your team to implement (just guess at a size at first). Give yourself plenty of padding. There will be plenty of time for stone-cold reality later. Bask in the glow of infinite possibilities for the moment.

If your estimates are too small (like days or weeks), you've slipped into detail land. Put those cards to one side and start over. If you can't imagine being able to estimate a story ("Easy to Use" is the classic example), put it to one side. Better yet, think about some specific things that would make the system easy to use, and turn them into stories (for example, "Personal Profiles").

You can only estimate from experience. What if you don't have any experience? Then you'd better fake it. Write a little prototype. Ask a friend who knows. Invite a programmer into the conversation.

Move fast. You're sketching here, trying to quickly capture a picture of the whole system. Don't spend more than a few hours on your first rough plan.

What, Me Worry?

Kent has a client that based its business plan on a set of big stories much like the ones above (different topic, naturally, since space travel seemed a bit dicey, even to venture capitalists). When the team began implementing the stories, they measured their progress at about 40 percent of the original plan.

Amazingly, this is perfectly okay! Nobody is happy that he or she is going slower than the plan, but the team's progress is not putting the company at risk. Far from it. Because they can demonstrate their progress regularly, and because they can react as the market changes, investors and customers believe the company will continue to do great things. About half the functionality actually implemented was in the original plan, and the other half has been brought in or invented in response to real customers.

Gotta love the Internet. Where else does accomplishing 20 percent of your original plan make you a superstar?

Chapter 10

Release Planning

In release planning the customer chooses a few months' worth of stories, typically focusing on a public release.

The big plan helped us decide that it wasn't patently stupid to invest in the project. Now we need to synchronize the project with the business. We have to synchronize two aspects of the project:

⬦ Date
⬦ Scope

Often, important dates for a project come from outside the company:

✧ The date on the contract
✧ COMDEX
✧ When the VC money will run out

Even if the date of the next release is internally generated, it will be set for business reasons. You want to release often to stay ahead of your competition, but if you release too often, you won't ever have enough new functionality to merit a press release, a new round of sales calls, or champagne for the programmers.

Release planning allocates user stories to releases and iterations—what should we work on first? what will we work on later? The strategies you will use are similar to making the big plan in the first place:

✧ Break the big stories into smaller stories.
✧ Sharpen the focus on the stories by estimating how long each will take.
✧ Defer less valuable stories until what is left fits in the time available.

Who Does Release Planning?

Release planning is a joint effort between the customer and the programmers. The customer drives release planning, and the programmers help navigate. The customer chooses which stories to place in the release and which stories to implement later, while the programmers provide the estimates required to make a sensible allocation.

The customer

✧ Defines the user stories
✧ Decides what business value the stories have
✧ Decides what stories to build in this release

The programmers

✧ Estimate how long it will take to build each story
✧ Warn the customer about significant technical risks
✧ Measure their team progress to provide the customer with an overall budget

How Stable Is the Release Plan?

Not at all.

The only thing we know for certain about a plan is that development won't go according to it. So release planning happens all the time. Every time the customer changes his mind about the requirements and his priority, this changes the plan. Every time the developers learn something new about the speed of doing things, this changes the plan.

The plan is therefore just a snapshot of the current view of what things will be done. This snapshot helps people get an idea of what to expect, but it is no statement of certainty. It will be revised frequently. Everyone—developers, customers, and management—needs to accept constant change.

How Far in Advance Do You Plan?

How far in advance do you build a release plan for? We know that the further ahead we plan, the less accurate we will be, so there's little point going into great detail for years into the future. We prefer to plan one or two iterations in advance and one or two releases in advance.

Focusing on one or two iterations means that the programmers clearly need to know what stories are in the iteration they are currently working on. It's also useful to know what's in the next iteration. Beyond that the iteration allocation is not so useful.

However, the business needs to know what is currently in this release, and it's useful to have an idea of what will be in the release after that.

The real decider for how far in advance you should plan is the cost of keeping the plan up-to-date versus the benefit you get when you know that plans are inherently unstable. You have to honestly assess the value compared to the volatility of the plans.

How Do You Plan Infrastructure?

When you plan in a function-oriented way, such as we suggest, the obvious question is how to deal with infrastructure. Before we can start building functionality we have to put together the distributed object messaging infrastructure, the database persistence infrastructure, and the dynamic GUI frameworks. This suggests a plan where you spend several months building the infrastructure components before you deliver any customer functionality.

This style of development is a common feature of the dead and dying projects we've seen—and we don't think it's a coincidence. Doing infrastructure without customer function leads to the following risks:

✧ You spend a lot of time not delivering things that are valuable to the customer, which strains the relationship with the customer.

✧ You try to make the infrastructure cover everything you think you might need, which leads to an overly complex infrastructure.

Therefore, evolve the infrastructure as you build the functionality. For each iteration, build just enough infrastructure for the stories in that iteration. You won't build a more complex infrastructure than you need, and the customer is engaged in building the infrastructure because she sees the dependent functionality as it's evolving.

How Do You Store the Release Plan?

Our preferred form of release plan is a set of cards. Each card represents a user story and contains the essential information to describe what the story is about. You group the cards together to show which stories are in this release. Lay out stories with adhesive on a wall, or pin them up on a cork board. Wrap future stories with a rubber band and stick them safely in a drawer.

We like cards because they are simple, physical devices that encourage everyone to manipulate them. It's always that little bit harder for people to see and manipulate things that are stored in a computer.

However, if you want to put your stories in a computer, go ahead. Just do it in a simple way. A simple spreadsheet often does the job best. People who use complicated project management packages are prone to spending time fiddling with the package when they should be communicating with other people.

Another computer format that many people are using is Wiki, a collaborative Web tool invented by Ward Cunningham (c2.com). Teams rapidly evolve conventions within Wiki's flexible format for recording stories, tasks, and status.

How Much Can You Put into a Release?

If you have stories, iterations, and releases, you need to know how many stories you can do in each iteration and release. We use the term

velocity to represent how much the team can do in an iteration. We measure the velocity of the team and estimate the amount of effort required for each story (see Chapter 12 for details on how we do this).

The sum of the effort for all the work you want to do cannot exceed the available effort. When you are planning an iteration, the sum of the story estimates cannot exceed the team's velocity. When you are planning a release, the sum of the story estimates cannot exceed the team's velocity times the number of iterations.

Release Planning Chapters

The next few chapters discuss the various elements of release planning in more detail.

- ✧ Chapter 11 discusses how to write stories so that you can break up the features of the system into useful chunks. It also talks about why the stories don't need to be too detailed.
- ✧ Chapter 12 talks about how to estimate how much time it will take to implement a story and how you can measure the team's velocity.
- ✧ Chapter 13 contains advice on the order in which you should implement your stories—do the high-value stories first but with half an eye on technical risks.
- ✧ Chapter 14 talks about the various events that cause you to do more release planning in the middle of a release.
- ✧ Chapter 15 talks about how to come up with the first plan, which is always both the hardest and the least accurate.
- ✧ Chapter 16 talks about common variations on the release planning process.

You'll notice that we begin by talking about how you plan in the middle of the project and later talk about how you come up with a first plan. You may find this frustrating as you probably will need a first plan first. But we noticed that with continuous planning, the first plan is actually quite an oddity. So XP makes later plans easier; the first plan is a special case.

Even though you start with a first plan, it's important to be familiar with what planning will look like when you get going. You'll find planning will get both easier and more accurate once you have a few iterations under your belt. If you have an idea of how the process should feel, you may find it easier to get over the inevitable initial bumps.

Chapter 11

Writing Stories

"Tell a me story."
—Every child at some point

The story is the unit of functionality in an XP project. We demonstate progress by delivering tested, integrated code that implements a story. A story should be understandable to customers and developers, testable, valuable to the customer, and small enough so that the programmers can build half a dozen in an iteration.

A user story is a chunk of functionality (some people use the word *feature*) that is of value to the customer. It provides a simple way for developers and customers to chop up what the system needs to do so the system can be delivered in pieces.

The emphasis on the word *simple* is essential. There are many books out there that go into great detail about requirements engineering, use case design, and similar topics. These present some useful ideas, but as ever XP looks for the simplest approach that could possibly work. So as we look at stories, remember that the whole point is to make them too simple to work in the hope that we might just get away with it.

Principles of Good Stories

Stories must be understandable to the customer. It's no good making the requirements so difficult to write and organize that you need years of training in requirements engineering to be able to understand them. The language for a story is plain English (or whatever your local language is). Everyone can speak natural language; anything else is just, um, unnatural.

We like to write user stories on index cards. Cards keep stories terse and also make them easy to manipulate during planning sessions. Developers and customers can pass a card back and forth, put it in a certain location on the table, put it back in the deck, pin it up on a cork board, and so forth. It is much easier to manipulate concepts on cards than it is to manipulate a printed list of items.

(If you're determined to put stories into a computer, do so in such a way that you can easily print them out on cards using standard printer card stock.)

The best user story is a sentence or two that describes something important to the customer. For example:

The system should check the spelling of all words entered in the comments field.

The shorter the story the better. The story represents a concept and is not a detailed specification. *A user story is nothing more than an agreement that the customer and developers will talk together about a feature.* Hideous written detail is not necessary if the customer can work with the programmers while they are programming. You are trying to reduce the probability of nasty surprises when the time comes to do the iteration plan and build the story.

It's not that you don't need all of those details. You just don't need them all up front. When you need to build the stories, then you need more details (see Chapter 17). But whatever you do to make the story more detailed, do it when you need the details. This leaves you with some uncertainty, but we've found that more detail doesn't ward off uncertainty, all it does is give the illusion of certainty—which we think is worse.

Each story must provide something of value to the customer. If the customer isn't getting value from an activity, why would he want to pay you to do it? Any technical infrastructure must be built in conjunction with the stories and must be developed to support what the stories need. This helps to avoid projects spending weeks or months providing clever infrastructure that isn't really needed.

Developers do not write user stories. Any "good idea" or "neat new feature" that a developer dreams up will not appear on a user story unless the customer agrees that the idea is good, or that the feature is neat. The customer has the sole responsibility for supplying the team with user stories, and no one can usurp this responsibility. Developers are welcome to suggest stories, but they should spend most of their attention on technical decisions.

One of the hardest things about stories is how big to make them. *Stories need to be of a size that you can build a few of them in each iteration.* This size gives you the ability to steer by shifting stories between iterations. It also means that the developers should be able to estimate how long it will take to do a story. If they can't, it usually means the story needs to be broken down into smaller parts.

The stories require communication between the customer and developers. The customer must write the story; the developers then estimate the story. The two parties must collaborate and communicate to do this.

Stories should be independent of each other. This allows us the freedom to build them in any order. This is, of course, impossible. But in practice we find that if we pretend it is possible, most of the time we get away with it. We do get dependencies, but rarely will they cause a problem with the planning process. If there's an effect that would change the estimates depending on what order the stories are done, then we can just write that on the card. We find we don't get many of them.

When the story gets built it will be important to be able to know that it works. *So each story must be testable.* You don't have to write the test right now, but you should be able to figure out how to test whether the story is there or not.

- -

Feedback from Estimation

In Chapter 12 we talk about how you estimate a story. You should start getting estimates as soon as you start writing stories. The main reason you want to do this is to get some feedback as to the right level of detail for estimation.

It is very common for a user to write a story that cannot be easily estimated. For example:

It should be easy for the user to diagnose a failure.

What does this mean? How can we estimate it? Because we don't know what it means, we cannot estimate it. Thus we ask the customer to explain what would make diagnosing a failure easy and what has made it hard in the past. We ask the customer to describe what operations she envisions that would make the process easy. For example:

Regardless of the state of the system, the user should be able to do something to the icon of a failed device that starts the diagnosis process.

The customer has made several things clear. First, "easy to diagnose" really means "easy to start the diagnosis process." Second, the customer envisions device icons on the screen. She also thinks it's important that the users be able to do things to those icons. This gives us enough context to estimate the story.

Programmers don't need infinite detail in order to estimate; they just need the customer to translate her needs into something concrete that they can take action on.

Prioritizing User Stories

It doesn't really help to ask for absolute rankings of stories such as high, medium, and low. All the stories end up being high or the customer wouldn't have written them, now would they? Instead, the customer needs to prepare to answer the question "What would you like us to implement first, and what will we implement later?"

Stories often mix priorities. For example:

Results must be displayed within 10 seconds and must contain the dispatch statement and all measured and derived readings.

What the customer really considers to be of high priority within the story is the appearance of the dispatch statement within 10 seconds. If it takes longer for the measured and derived readings to appear, that's not a problem. Under the press of limited time though, the customer will discover what's important and what isn't.

It is almost impossible to find this kind of baggage early on. What usually happens is that the programmers will challenge the priority of individual elements of a story during iteration planning, or even development. Once the baggage is detected, regardless of when, the story can be split.

Traceability

Eventually the customer will have to specify acceptance tests whose execution will determine whether the user stories have been successfully implemented. Thus all user stories must be testable. The programmers and the customer alike must agree that there are concrete tests that will demonstrate that the user story has been successfully implemented.

Acceptance testing is also our answer to traceability. We don't think it's worth trying to trace requirements to classes in the system that implement the requirement. That's too much paperwork. Even if you have a tool, it's still too much effort to keep all the information consistent. Instead, we prefer the simpler trace between story and the acceptance tests. If the acceptance tests work, we can safely assume that some code exists that maps to the story. If we change that code later in such a way that breaks the story, then the test will fail. This is the ultimate in traceability.

Splitting User Stories

Splitting a user story into two or more smaller user stories is extremely common. The mechanism is simple: The customer divides the concept into two or more smaller concepts, writes the new cards, and throws the old card away. The developers then estimate the new stories, and the customers prioritize them.

The dispatch statement must be displayed within 10 seconds.

All measured and derived readings must be displayed within 30 seconds.

Many events can trigger a split.

✧ When you're writing the initial stories the developers may say that a story is too large.
✧ When you're doing release planning you find you cannot fit all of a story into an iteration. Then you can split the story so that part of it can be done in the iteration.
✧ As you're tracking an iteration you realize you have too much to do.

To split a story a customer begins by suggesting a split. The customer should make the split along priority lines, factoring out some less vital work that can wait till the next iteration. Once the customer has made the trial split, the developers then estimate the two parts as if they were separate stories.

Of course, this is not likely to work out just right the first time. If the split leaves the lower-priority part too small, the customer needs to move more work into the lower-priority piece. If the low-priority piece is too big, the customer may move some work to the higher-priority piece or he could leave it as it is and move some other work into the iteration to make up for the difference.

You'll go back and forth a few times on this, but if everyone is in the room together it won't take too long to get a feel for what makes stories good.

User Story Adornments

We prefer to keep our user stories uncluttered. They contain only three pieces of data: the name, the story itself, and estimates. There is no doubt that other data items could be invented. The list of possibilities is nearly endless. But we recommend that you refrain from "wouldn't it be nice ifs" and "it might be convenient ifs." Uncluttered stories written on a card are easy to manipulate, and will save time and effort compared to the cost of the occasional lack of convenient data.

The Story Writing Process

It is tempting to write a simple little cookbook, *Great User Stories in Just 30 Minutes*. It would make your customer's job much easier. All except that part where we can't do it—any more than you can write a cookbook for great literary storytelling. The best we can do is tell you how to spot bad stories and suggest that you spend a lot of time going back and forth between customer and programmer while you're feeling your way.

The process of writing stories is iterative, requiring lots of feedback. Customers will propose a story to the programmers. The programmers will ask themselves if the story can be tested and estimated, and if it is of appropriate size. If the story cannot be estimated, the programmers will ask the customer to clarify the story. If the story is too big, the developers will ask the customer to split the story.

Stories should be written a few at a time. The programmers should sit down with the customer, figure out between two and five stories, and then stop. The programmers then estimate those stories. While the programmers are estimating, they will certainly want to talk to the customer about the details and issues. So the programmers and the customer are in constant communication.

In some cases the estimates may be obvious. Perhaps the story is similar to others that have already been completed. In other cases the story may be very difficult to estimate and may require exploratory programming. Such exploration rarely takes longer than a day, and you should always rewrite any code that you wrote while doing the exploratory programming.

Once the first few stories have been estimated, the programmers and the customer will have a better understanding of what makes for good stories. An image of the system is beginning to form in her mind. From this superior viewpoint, the customer is ready to write the next few stories and repeat the process.

Don't be too impressed with your stories. Writing the stories is not the point. Communicating is the point. We've seen too many requirements documents that are written down but don't involve communication.

When Are You Done Writing Stories?

Never, or at least not until the project is cancelled. Software projects grow and change over time. While story writing will be most prolific during the early phases of the project, it will never end.

When have you done enough user stories to begin developing? When the customer is certain that the most important stories have been identified and you have enough stories for several months' worth of development. There should be enough stories so the customer can make meaningful choices.

Everyone (especially at the beginning of projects) needs to feel heard. If the customer needs to write (quickly write) two years' worth of stories before he feels listened to, so be it. Get it over with quickly, make the stories as big as possible, then focus back in on what you should work on first, and what will have to wait.

Usually the start of the project is characterized by a lot of story writing as you try to get a broad feel of the desired functionality of the system. The list of stories will drive the initial release plan.

However the initial stories are only a start. As the project goes on stories will be added, dropped, and split all the time. Not only is this normal; it is the whole point of XP. The aim is to deliver software that matches the requirements at every release, not to match the requirements as they were misunderstood at the beginning of the project.

The Disposition of User Stories

Once a user story has been implemented and its acceptance tests are running, the story itself serves no further purpose. Members of the development team might think of tiling their floors or papering their walls with story cards; but discarding them is probably the best option. Remember that the stories are encoded in far more detail and accuracy in the acceptance tests, so no information will be lost if the cards themselves are destroyed.

Stories

One of the problems about talking about stories is giving examples. We can't usually show examples from real projects because of client confidentiality. This presents a bit of a problem.

For this book, however, we got lucky. Kent was clearing some trees from his farm in Oregon when he came across a reverse time capsule. The capsule contained project information about a travel booking project that we did in the twenty-fourth century. (Or is that "will do"? trans-temporal tense can get very confusing.)

Among the things inside this time capsule were story cards for the project.

Find lowest fare.

Present to the customer the ten lowest fares for a particular route.

Show available flights.

Show possible flights (with connections) between any two planets.

Sort available flights by convenience.

When you're showing the flights, sort them by convenience: time of journey, number of changes, closeness to desired departure and arrival time.

Purchase ticket.

Purchase ticket charging to a credit card. Check credit card validity when doing this. Also check broad immigration rules (no Oolavoos to go to Traal etc.)

Do customer profile.

Keep customer details for quick reference, for example, credit card info, home address, dietary and gravitational needs.

Review itineraries.

Show all itineraries the customer has in the system.

Cancel itinerary.

If a customer cancels an itinerary, cancel all flights, hotels, etc.

Print immigration paperwork.

Print paperwork required to leave and arrive at a planet—only for the easier planets (e.g., not Vogon).

Show hotels.

Show hotels near a place.

Show hotel availability.

Show hotels that are available for the period indicated by the itinerary.

Offer sophisticated hotel search.

Allow customer to search for hotels using more than dates and location. This would include facilities, level of service, costs, and recommendations.

Book a hotel.

Book a hotel. Charge to credit card and check credit card validity.

Provide hotel/spaceline programs.

Show hotels that have joint sales agreements with the spaceline the customer is using. Show the prices including the discounts that are available with these programs—only for spacelines that are actively collaborating with us at this stage.

Offer airplane hire.

Allow the customer to hire an airplane while he or she is on a planet. Link the dates in from the space flight. Enhance the customer profile to include airplane preferences (insurance selection, manual versus automatic, etc.)

The stories show by example the principles we've discussed so far. Each one is short, too short to act as a detailed specification for programming. However, they give enough information to provide a common expectation. For anyone who has used a Web-based travel reservation system, the stories do give a good picture of what is needed at each stage. For people without that background, you may well need a little more information, but we should still avoid great detail at this stage.

Notice how there is no discussion at all of dependencies. You could well argue that to "Offer sophisticated hotel search" you would need to do "Show hotel availability." The order in which you tackle them might affect the estimates. But essentially we don't worry about it. If order does make a significant difference to the estimates, and that has an effect on the planning process, then a simple note will do the trick.

Chapter 12

Estimation

Base your story estimates on a similar story you've already done. This story will take about the same amount of time as a comparable story.

How do you come up with estimates? We've seen a lot of words devoted to this topic. We've seen quite a few mathematical formulae. The best of these are based on the lines of code yet to be written. These can tell you how much time it will take to develop so many thousand lines of code. This is particularly useful since it's so easy to estimate precisely how many lines of code a solution will require before you start writing it. (Spotted the sarcasm yet?)

Let's be clear, estimation is an art at best. You're not going to get accurate figures however hard you try. With a little bit of effort you can, however, get good enough numbers, and you can get better numbers over time.

There are three keys to effective estimation:

◇ Keep it simple.
◇ Use what happened in the past.
◇ Learn from experience.

The best guide to estimating the future is to look for something that happened in the past that was about the same as the future thing. Then just assume that history will repeat itself. It often does. If there's a significant difference between then and now, then use a very simple way to factor it in. Don't try to be too sophisticated; estimates will never be anything other than approximate, however hard you try.

Estimating the Size of a Story

A simple, effective way to estimate the size of a story is to look for a similar story that you've already delivered. Then look at your records to see how long it took to build. Then assume the new story will take the same amount of effort. "Oh, another report. Reports always take us a week."

If you can't find a story that is the same size, look for something half as big or twice as big. Multiply or divide as appropriate. Do not worry that Martin probably failed to get an A in his Further Maths A level because of his unfortunate habit of multiplying by two when he should have divided. You're a lot cleverer than he is.

It doesn't actually matter what units you express the estimate in. The only important thing is that you always use the same unit. In this book we use ideal weeks. Ideal weeks are the number of person weeks that the story would take to implement if the programmers could dedicate 100 percent of their time to it.

(You'll notice a slight flaw in this approach. How do you estimate when you haven't built anything yet and you don't have anything to compare it to? See Chapter 15 for a thoroughly unsatisfactory solution to this problem.)

Estimation is a team effort. The team discusses the story, considers how long it may take to implement, and decides upon an estimate. The team members may disagree regarding the estimate. Some may think the story is hard and will take a long time to develop. Others may think it is easy and will take a short time to develop. We follow the rule "Optimism wins." That is, if after reasonable discussion the disagreement persists, we choose the shortest estimate.

Remember, estimates are not commitments. And a couple of bad estimates are not disasters. What we are aiming for is to continuously improve our ability to make estimates. By choosing the most optimistic estimate we accomplish two things: We keep tension in the estimates so that they don't grow hideously long, and we keep tension in the team so that the team learns not to be too optimistic. Team members whose optimism burned the team once will learn to temper that optimism.

Another issue that worries many people is dependencies between the stories. As we say in Chapter 13, you can mostly ignore dependencies. However, mostly doesn't mean always. You will get some cases where you say "Flooping the thingummy will take six weeks, but if we do it after we burble the foobar it'll take only four weeks." In this case use the appropriate number for flooping depending on its position and make a note of the assumption. You will have only a few of these.

Periodically you will reestimate every story, which gives you a chance to incorporate additional information such as dependencies that have been erased or technologies that turn out to be difficult (or easy, we suppose).

Estimating How Much You Can Do in an Iteration

You can think of each iteration as a box, each of which can hold a limited number of wine bottles. The key question to any oenophile is how many bottles can you fit in a box? You could measure the box, measure the bottles and do some geometric analysis, you could form a committee of august persons, or you could just try it and see.

We use the latter approach: Yesterday's Weather. At the end of each iteration we measure how much stuff got done and assume we'll get the same work done this time. However, when we talked about Yesterday's Weather, we just talked about the general principle. To apply it to release planning we need to figure out how to measure the stuff. We could just count the number of stories we do, but not all stories are the same size.

So we have to measure the size of each story. At the end of each iteration we look at all the stories that got done, and we record how many weeks of ideal time it took to do each story. We then add up all the ideal time in all the stories, and that tells us how much ideal time there is in each iteration.

Following this simple rule violates one of the dictums of project management: Work expands to fill the available space. That may be true for some activities, but it isn't true when you have motivated and capabable software developers.

Be wary of adjusting velocity to cope with changes in a team's size. As we discussed in Chapter 7, changing the composition of a team has a nonlinear and delayed effect on velocity. Don't predict the effect; measure it. Predicting the effect of adding people is particularly difficult, because you rarely know how long it will take for the new people to begin helping.

We also use velocity for individual developers. We might say that one programmer has a velocity of 5 ideal days. That means that that programmer can sign up for 5 ideal days of work in each iteration. Most developers will have the same velocity. However, someone working part-time, or someone who is new to the team, will have a lower velocity.

You have to be careful not to attach too much meaning to velocity. Say you have two teams of the same size with the same iteration lengths but different velocities. What does this mean?

The answer is all sorts of things tangled up together. It might mean one team is more talented or that one team had better tools. But it might also mean that one team tended to use more optimistic estimates than the other and needed a smaller velocity to compensate. In the end, all of this stuff about ideal time is one almighty fudge to compensate for the difficulty of estimating software development.

The Meaning of Ideal Time

There's been a fair bit of discussion in the XP community about what units of effort we should use.

In many ways, the simplest unit would be calendar effort, which is based on calendar time.

Calendar time is the familiar passage of time, modified to handle working days. If you are working Mondays to Fridays, then four calendar weeks is equal to 20 calendar days.

Calendar effort is the number of people times calendar time. A team of six people has 30 calendar development days of effort available per calendar week. In four weeks they would have 24 calendar development weeks of effort available. If one person on the team worked half-time, the team would have 22 calendar development weeks of effort available in that same four-week period.

Most people measure all tasks in terms of calendar effort. This makes sense because it's easy to measure. However, it makes estimating harder. Estimating is much simpler if you think of people as working at reasonable efficiency. Typically this means they don't get interrupted and distracted. Distractions tend to even out over the long haul but can have a big effect in short periods of a week or two. As such they really make a mess of historical data, which is the backbone of a good estimation system.

So in XP we come up with a second kind of time: ideal time. **Ideal time** is time without interruption where you can concentrate on your work and you feel fully productive. We measure and estimate using ideal time, because that allows us to compare tasks without worrying about interruptions. If we look at a task and see it is about as complicated as one that took two ideal days last week, we can estimate it will take two ideal days this week. The elapsed time could well be very different, but that is something we monitor separately.

We use the term "ideal time," but really it's ideal effort. A team of six people might have ten ideal development days of effort available a week. Typically when people talk of task lengths they say, "That'll take three ideal days." What they really mean is that it will take "three ideal development days," but that's too much of a mouthful.

The notion of ideal time has little to do with time. Indeed some people like to use something like story points, task points, or Gummi Bears to measure the effort for stories and tasks. This works because the only important thing is that you use the same unit for the actual stories you measured in the past as you use for your estimates today.

(Francesco Cirillo told us he bought a half-hour kitchen timer in the shape of a tomato, so they now refer to a "six-tomato task.")

We like using ideal weeks because the concept has some correspondence to the familiar, yet the word *ideal* is there to remind us that things aren't perfect. It also can help early on when doing your first plan (Chapter 15).

Ideal time is the time you spend on tasks you have accepted responsibility for. Ideal time doesn't include time you spend helping someone else, such as pair programming. You might think you need to take explicit account of time spent not programming, but it turns out Yesterday's Weather takes care of tracking how much time you spend on your own tasks.

(If you've read some older stuff on XP you'll come across the term **load factor.** Load factor is the ratio of the calendar effort in an iteration to velocity. So a team with five people using two-week iterations has ten elapsed programming weeks per iteration. If the team's velocity is four then the team has a load factor of 2.5 (10/4). We used to use load factor a lot in planning, but since then we have learned that it's easier to just use velocity.)

Improving Your Estimates

The good news about the estimation process is that it tends to improve. As you do it more often, as you build up more acutal figures, everyone on the team gets better at estimation. Encourage this process. Don't expect too much of early estimates, but do expect them to improve.

For this to work you need to track your actuals. Make sure you record how long it took to do a story. The record shouldn't be any more precise than your planning precision, so estimating to the nearest ideal week will be fine. Building up a good set of actuals is essential to improving the planning process.

Chapter 13

Ordering the Stories

The most important stories to do first are the ones that contain the highest business value. Beware of sequencing stories based on technical dependencies. Most of the time the dependencies are less important than the value.

One of the key parts of planning is deciding in what order you should do things. There is never any shortage of things to do. What should we do today?

Sometimes software is just too complicated, so instead let's consider something that is both more mundane and more essential. In cooking you answer this question by looking at the timing and sequencing in the recipe. Often there is quite a strong ordering involved: You have to fry the onions golden before you put in the chicken.

This notion of ordering is the dominant aspect of most kinds of planning. On big engineering projects this is what leads to the practice of dependency analysis and PERT charts. Dependencies between tasks dominate planning. Your mission, should you choose to accept it, is to find the best way of navigating through the dependencies.

To plan in this style you need to lay out a list of tasks and capture the dependencies between the activities. By looking at these and looking at the duration of the activities you can figure out the key activities on the critical path where a delay will affect the whole project. If you do a course on project management you'll usually spend a good bit of time on this kind of analysis, together with such topics as resource leveling. You may well use a computer tool to help deal with all of this.

All of these techniques are pretty much useless on an XP project. They are useless because dependencies between tasks do not figure strongly, because of the emphasis on minimal technical commitment and constant growth in the design. Most of the time there is no necessary ordering between the stories. You can build them in any order you like. We don't have proof of this, but, like most software pundits, that never stopped us from making a brave assertion. Our evidence is simply that nearly every time someone comes up with an ordering constraint, we can shoot it down.

A good example is a project Martin ran into for doing costing analysis for a factory system. The cost models were complicated and very new, so they were not well understood. They ran on a large amount of data. The project team reasoned that since the models needed the data, the software to enter the data needed to be written first. This meant building a lot of GUI screens for entering and validating the data.

That was a false dependency. The data could have been put into the database using raw SQL. This method would have allowed them to work with the costing models and figure out what the models were really about. Until they understood the models better, they didn't know what data they needed. Running the models was the point of the application after all, the data was there only to serve the models.

Most ordering dependencies are false. Of course, most isn't all. The cases where you do get dependencies, they are easy to deal with on a case by case basis, either inside an iteration where you have control or by modifying estimates midstream. They don't affect the overall plan much.

A logical, yet naïve, reader would see this lack of constraints as a benefit. But often it isn't. Instead, we see people who are looking for dependencies and are so determined to find them that they find dependencies that don't exist. After all, if there is no ordering constraint, how do we choose in what order to do things?

Business Value

So we need different factors for making our choice. The first of these is business value. Do those stories first that yield the most benefit to the customers. This seems so obvious that we hardly feel the need to point out why. But just in case, we'll do it anyway.

We want to get a release to the customer as soon as possible. We want this release to be as valuable to the customer as possible. That way the customer will like us and keep feeding us cookies. So we give her the things she wants most. That way we can release quickly and the customer feels the benefit. Should everything go to pot at the end of the schedule, it's okay, because the stories at risk are less important than the stories we have already completed.

Even if we can't release quickly, the customer will be happier if we do the most valuable things first. It shows we are listening, and really trying to solve her problems. It also may prompt the customer to go for an earlier release once she sees the value of what appears. Early releases scare people who do prototyping, because prototypes aren't production quality. But XP never builds anything it can't be proud of, so we can deliver at any moment.

How do we measure the business value of a story? The short answer is that we don't; that is, the developers and project managers don't. Determining business value is a decision entirely within the realm of the business people. It's their business; they know what the value is. At least, they are better positioned to guess than we are. If they're wrong, well, they're paying for it. If you have enough dollars you have the right to be wrong. The developers can suggest alternatives and ask questions. But in the end business value is always a business call.

How carefully should you figure out the value of stories? You don't need to get it to the dollar; indeed, it usually isn't worth trying to put a dollar value on it at all. The relative values are what counts, and you need only a rough sense of the relativity.

This is enough to start with. As you play out the release plan, you'll allocate the stories into iterations, and that will lead to a finer determination of business value. But in order to do that the business needs some more information.

Imagine you're standing in front of the new car that you've been salivating over for years. Finally the old heap has thrown a rod and you can reward yourself with a year of that new car smell. You're finalizing the deal and the salesman asks, "Would you like the optional sunroof with that, sir?" What do you answer?

Unless you're either incredibly cheap or incredibly rich (or incredibly against fresh air) you'll want one piece of information: How much is that window in the Rover? If the cost is $10 you'd probably take it. If it's $10,000 you'll probably pass. But if the range is that big, you can't decide without the cost.

For most software, the range is that big.

So who gets to allocate the cost? Developers state the cost, and they state it by estimating how much effort it will take (see Chapter 12).

Technical Risk

As the developers look at the stories they will inevitably start thinking about how they will build them. As they do this they will run the gamut of feelings, all the way from "no problem" to "can't be done." These feelings are important, because they are the manifestation of where the project could go off the rails. When developers feel nervous, everyone should listen.

The nervousness comes from a number of sources:

◆ The developers may not be confident that they can estimate the story to the required precision.
◆ A story may depend on an untrusted third-party piece of software.
◆ The developers may not know how to make the whole system fast enough for future loads.
◆ The developers may not know how to design today so an expected feature can be added without reworking most of the system.

In general, programmers want to do higher-risk stories first. That way, if something goes wrong, you find out early while you still have time to deal with it.

Negotiating Between the Two

You notice we have two different criteria set by two different groups of people. How do we resolve the two of them? Programmers want to tackle high-risk stories first, and customers want to tackle high-value stories first. There are plenty of times when these conflicting priorities have to be resolved.

Business should sequence stories. Business people understand uncertainty in estimates. They face risk all the time with financial projections. They also understand the cost of reworking in the cases where reworking is an issue. If they wish to run a risk in order to get better value now, it is really their call. It is the programmers' task to make the risk visible, not to make the decision for the customer.

While this arrangement is the ideal, sometimes you need something extra to make it work, perhaps allowing developers to choose a certain amount of stories per iteration so that they can bring the risk forward.

We need to stress that you shouldn't worry too much about the issue of reworking. XP's practices are all about reducing the cost of reworking to manageable levels. If you find yourself in a situation where the cost of reworking is prohibitive, then you should either not use XP or you should use an environment that makes rework easier.

We'll confess that we disagree a little on this. Martin is much more inclined to bring stories forward due to risk than Kent is. Kent considers Martin a coward for this attitude. Martin agrees.

Example Release Plan

Let's take a look at the release plan from the time capsule. The information was annotated on the cards, but we've transposed it all into a handy table for you (see Table 13.1).

We measured the team's velocity at six ideal weeks per iteration. As you can see, stories have been assigned to iterations. There's a release after the first two iterations and a further release two iterations later. (The releases are a little short, but this is enough for an example. And in any case, there's this confidentiality agreement that prohibits us from showing the whole plan two centuries before we begin.)

There are a few things worth noting:

- ✧ The "Do customer profile" story has been split up into two parts with different priorities. The estimates don't add up in this case. Often they do, but from time to time they don't. That's not an error. Each story should be estimated independently, so it does happen. Maybe breaking it apart made us realize it was bigger than we thought, or maybe doing them separately would take longer. The reason usually isn't important, so there's no need to document it.
- ✧ The second iteration only has five ideal weeks of stories assigned to it even though the velocity is six. That's okay—additional work, either new stories or pieces of later stories, may well get added closer to the iteration's date.
- ✧ A note on the card for "Show hotel availability" indicates that the estimate depends on other work. That's not uncommon, but it

TABLE 13.1 Time Capsule Release Plan

Story	Time Estimate (Ideal Weeks)	Assigned Iteration #	Assigned Release #
Find lowest fare.	3	2	1
Show available flights.	2	1	1
Sort available flights by convenience.	4		2
Purchase ticket.	2	1	1
Do customer profile.	4		
Do simple customer profile.	2	1	1
Do full customer profile.	3		
Review itineraries.	1	2	1
Cancel itinerary.	2		2
Print immigration paperwork.	4		
Show hotels.	3		2
Show hotel availability.	2[a]		2
Offer sophisticated hotel search.	3		
Book a hotel.	1	2	1
Provide hotel/spaceline programs.	3		
Offer airplane hire.	3		

a. Is 4 if "Show hotels" isn't already there

isn't worth making a fuss about. It was probably only recorded as the customer was figuring out what to put in iteration 2.

⬧ It may look odd that "Book a hotel" is assigned to iteration 2 when "Show hotels" isn't assigned yet. How can you book a hotel if you can't see the list? The point here is that the functionality won't be available to the user yet but will be built into the system and can be functionally tested to the satisfaction of the customer. Not all behavior has to be usable by the user to be included in the iteration; the key criteria is that it is testable. You'll often find this in cases where you need to build functionality in the core business logic but don't add the user interface until a later iteration.

⬧ You'll notice there are no details about the iteration length or size of team. This is deliberate to point out that you actually don't need that information for the basic release plan. All you need is the estimated stories and the velocity. Obviously you'll need the current date and the iteration length to tell people when an iteration will be done. Something along these lines as shown in Table 13.2.

TABLE 13.2 Iteration Completion Dates

Event	Date
Start	1 Apr. 29
Release 1 Complete	19 Apr. 29
Release 2 Complete	10 May 29

✧ It's comforting to know that even in the twenty-fourth century people will be using two digits for the year.

Chapter 14

Release Planning Events

Life is what happens to you while you're busy making other plans.
—John Lennon

Various events cause the team to do a little release planning. The customer adds and changes the priorities of stories, developers estimate stories, and the team notices if it has too much or too little to do.

As you are doing release planning, you'll find there are several things you need to do. In this chapter we talk about the various events in release planning and how you react to them.

Changing the Priorities of Stories

Businesses often change their priorities. By only committing to one iteration's worth of stories at a time the customer is guaranteed a chance to make priority decisions based on up-to-the-minute information about the priority and cost of the stories.

Adding a Story

If you compare XP to many of the other methodologies out there, the biggest difference to customers is that they don't have to commit to a detailed specification of everything they want before development begins. Requirements creep is perfectly reasonable and rational, even valuable. The requirements can creep wherever they like as long as we know where they are going and the customer is informed of the consequences. Indeed, we encourage the requirements to crawl around and find whatever it is the customer needs.

The customer can add a new story at any time. He writes the story as we describe in Chapter 11. Development then estimates the story in ideal effort. Now the customer can pick the story for any iteration, subject to the usual rule that the sum of the estimates of the stories for an iteration cannot exceed the velocity of the team. The customer moves stories as much as he likes to make room for the new story.

Rebuild the Release Plan

Most of the things we talk about are small-scale changes to a plan. You have to defer a few stories, move some stories about. Little changes like this keep the plan in good shape, but sometimes you need something a good bit more significant.

You need to rebuild the plan in the following circumstances:

✧ When the pile of deferred stories has grown too high. A few stories deferred till later is not worth rebuilding for, but if enough of them mount up that you are sure you aren't going to get everything done, it's time to do something about it.

✧ If the team's velocity changes, then all the assumptions for the release plan are broken and you need a new release plan.

A rebuild begins with development reestimating the stories. The original estimates were a good guess at the time. Since then everyone will have learned. A rebuild is a good time to take this learning into account. During the reestimating, developers can use the actual figures from recent stories to better calibrate their estimates. Reestimating is particularly important early in development as the early release plans will be the least accurate.

Once development has reestimated the stories, the customer picks a pile of stories that will fit. Just hold your nose and do the math. If you are running at around 8 weeks' worth of stories per iteration and you have three iterations to go, then the customer picks 24 weeks' worth of stories for this release. He will get the rest of the stories as soon after the release as possible.

You should expect to rebuild the plan every three or four iterations. You don't want to do it all the time, as it takes a fair amount of time, but it does need doing regularly. Think of it as changing the oil. You don't *have* to do it, but you'd be stupid not to.

Chapter 15

The First Plan

The first plan is the hardest and least accurate part of release planning. Fortunately you only have to do it once.

Making the First Plan

So now you know what a release plan looks like and how you use it. It should be clear that the accuracy of the plan depends on the accuracy of its estimates, and the accuracy of the estimates depends on the history of the project. The first plan has no history, so your estimates are flaky. What does this make the first plan?

Flaky. (Think Kramer with too much coffee.)

But you still need a plan to even get started. The plan gives you something to track against so you can assess progress. It gives you a framework of stories that allow you to notice what happens and build up the history to make the later plans better. The first plan, however, is always high on expectations and usually low on delivery.

The first plan has two main areas of uncertainty: the velocity of the team and size of the stories. Here are a few tips on how to do the best you can under the circumstances.

Velocity is measured. You won't get a decent picture of velocity until several iterations into the project. Before you can measure, the best you can do is guess.

One way to guess velocity is to measure progress while you are writing and estimating the first stories. During exploration, use tasks much along the lines of an iteration plan. Monitor progress and track the ideal time people report, much as you do with iteration tracking. See how much ideal time people get done and use that as a basis. Every time a programmer says, "I'll get that done in a day," notice how long it actually takes. If "a day's worth of work" generally takes three days on the calendar, then you could guess the team's velocity as number people × weeks/iteration/3.

If there's a similar project in your organization, you could use the team's velocity to help estimate yours. They have six people on three-week iterations. That's 18 calendar weeks per iteration. Their velocity is six. You have four people and are doing two-week iterations. That's eight calendar programming weeks per iteration. So a guess at your velocity is $6 \times 8/18$ which is about 2.

Story estimates are tough at first. The approach we've had the best luck with is to get the team to start with the stories they feel the most comfortable estimating. To estimate those first few stories, have people ask themselves, "If this story was all I had to do, and I had no distractions, how long do I think it would take?" Once they have done the comfortable stories, do the others by comparison, much as you would with historical estimates.

You may have another team that's done similar work. How can you use that experience? Don't get them to estimate the stories for you. That breaks the rule that those who do should be those who estimate. Being held to someone else's estimates will lead to lack of commitment and falling morale. Don't do that.

You can have your team look at the history of the other team and come up with its own gauge based on that. But you have to be careful not to let comparisons get too sticky. Once you start reasoning about how fast one team is compared with another you'll get all sorts of emotional reactions that will distort everyone's thinking. It can be helpful in flushing out all the issues that may come up. It can also be handy in comparing effort between tasks: "It took them half as much again to get the objects hooked into the relational database, so let's start with the same proportions for us."

Choosing Your Iteration Length

How long should an iteration be? There are a lot of people who favor iterative development, but they don't all answer this question the same way. Some people say that an iteration can be as long as six months. We go in the other direction. Iterations should be short—between one and three weeks. We favor two, and a recent survey on the XP eGroup (http://www.egroups.com/group/extremeprogramming) showed that two and three weeks were the most popular choices.

TABLE 15.1   Question: How Long Do Your Iterations Last?[a]

Choices	Votes	Percent
<1 week	0	0%
1 week	7	19%
2 weeks	14	38%
3 weeks	12	32%
4 weeks	3	8%
1 month	1	3%
>1 month	0	0%

a. Based on 37 replies

Why make them so short? One of the key things we want from a plan is an indication of progress: how far have we come, how far have we to go? Iterative development helps us judge progress, because each iteration delivers working, tested code—which is hard to fudge. But milestones only occur at the end of an iteration. The longer the iteration, the more risk you run of sliding just a little bit out of control. You want each iteration to be as short as possible, so that you know where you are as frequently as possible.

But there is such a thing as too short. Each iteration implies some overhead:

✧ Making sure the acceptance tests are running
✧ Planning the iteration
✧ Reporting to management

We don't want the overhead to be bigger than what we are trying to do in the iteration. If it is, we will stop planning and iterating.

Don't get too hung up about choosing the right iteration length. The world isn't going to end if you pick three-week iterations instead of two-week iterations. As long as you are prepared to be aware of the effects of iteration length, and prepared to experiment when you spot a problem, you can start most anywhere. So start with two-week iterations.

A related question is when do you start the iterations. We've been surprised by how many teams don't start on Monday. As one of Kent's clients so eloquently put it, "Mondays suck. Planning sucks. Why put them together?" This client starts iterations on Tuesday, and has been happy with the choice. Team members can spend the last Monday of the iteration tidying up, readying demos, and writing even more tests. The next day, they are ready to go.

Getting Started

Once you have the plan, how do you get started programming? You can't very well divide up the work if there's only one class.

We've had success in a big room with a projector connected to the computer. Bring the whole team—programmers, customers, and managers. Spend a couple of days implementing test cases, satisfying them, and evolving the design. At the end of that time you should have enough pieces that three or four pairs can work independently.

Another idea (thanks to Michael Hill) for getting started is the zero functionality iteration. There are often a bunch of little technical infrastructure tasks to get done before you can begin programming:

◇ Getting the testing framework working
◇ Getting the automated build structure working
◇ Getting the network up and running with all the appropriate permissions
◇ Getting the basic install scripts set up

You'd hate to commit to functionality in a first iteration only to disappoint the customer because you couldn't get the framdoozle talking to the whatzit. If you haven't worked with your technology before, consider spending two weeks getting the mechanism working just right before you begin programming.

Chapter 16

Release Planning Variations

Some local adaptations of the release planning are shorter releases, longer releases, and shorter stories.

Everywhere XP is adopted, it undergoes rapid evolution (see Chapter 27). Here are a few variations we have encountered.

Short Releases

Sometimes you can release much more often, maybe every iteration. This can happen for in-house development and also for application service providers where your users are distant but using thin clients and you have close control over the server.

Most of this is good news. Each iteration is ready for production, and going into production with each iteration is perfectly feasible. This usually means that you need to have high confidence in your tests and a very automated build process, but if you are doing XP you should have these anyway.

With short releases you don't really need any notion of a release at all. You can work iteration to iteration, planning one or two iterations ahead. This allows you to be very responsive to the customer, giving the customer control of the process with rapid feedback to see the results.

However, there is a danger to never having "a release." The customer may lose strategic vision of where the software needs to go. In this case the customer spends so much time choosing features for the short term that she misses important long-term needs.

The release can come back as a longer-term milestone. By the end of the next quarter we hope to be here, and by the end of the following quarter we want to be there. So even if you release into production every iteration, still think about planning out a release on a quarterly scale. Even though the resulting plan isn't very helpful as a predictor of the future, the act of planning those longer releases is vital. (Didn't some general say something like that?)

Long Releases

What happens if you can only release once a year?

Our first reaction to this reality is to question it. Maybe there is some way to release more frequently.

A common case for long releases is in replacing an existing system. Because you have to do all the things the old system had to do, you can't release something with only some of the features.

In this case look for a way to let the old and the new coexist. Manage some contracts with the old system and some with the new, gradually moving the contracts over with each release. This may involve extra work to migrate data between the systems and to integrate the user interfaces, but the resulting drop in risk is usually worth it.

Another case is with shrink-wrap software. Many users just will not want to upgrade their software every quarter, nor will the marketing department cope with the resulting flux. In this case look for a way to send intermediate releases to those customers that may be more interested in these versions. Call them service packs or something. That way at least some of your users will use the system in production, and you'll get the feedback you need.

Frequent releases are good, but if you can't release frequently you don't have to abandon XP completely. You may need to create interim releases that are only available internally. These will be enough for the friendly users to play with in controlled conditions and to provide a focus for planning purposes.

Small Stories

Some teams like to have more smaller stories. Instead of four or five two-week stories, they will plan 25 two-day stories. This gives the customer finer control over the activities of the team, at the cost of some of the flexibility of the team and more involvement by the customer.

Spatial Reasoning

James Goebel sent this story:

Interface Systems' Java Factory has a situation where there is a product manager responsible for planning long-term releases, a consulting team that generates short-term requirements based on customer needs, and a customer service manager who is responsible for qualifying product bugs and scheduling their repairs.

In order to accommodate these multiple voices we created a few simple tools. The first obvious tool is that each story card now lists the sponsoring customer so that programmers can easily remember with whom to talk when a question arises. The second tool we created is a game table for the planning game that has for each iteration a number of 8.5" x 11" open positions equal to the number of two-week stories that can be fit into the next two-week iteration.

After all the stories have been estimated by the team, a copy of the physical story card is sized proportionally to all the other story cards: three-week stories are 8.5" x 16", two-week stories are 8.5" x 11", one-week stories are 8.5" x 5.5", half-week stories are 8.5" x 2.75", and so on. The "committee customer" then meets to decide how to organize the story pieces on the playing board. By sizing the pieces so that all math can be done quickly using visual inspection, this meeting can remain focused on the competing business issues where the resulting release plan can be completed in only a couple of hours. This same game table remains available throughout the iteration cycle so that if a new story is created that requires immediate attention, the same "committee customer" can quickly decide how to adjust the plan to accommodate the reassignment of resources.

Chapter 17

Iteration Planning

Each iteration is planned by breaking down the stories for that iteration into tasks. Tasks are scheduled by asking programmers to sign up for the tasks they want, then asking them to estimate their tasks, then rebalancing as necessary.

The release plan is synchronized to the rhythms of business. It gives the business people a way of thinking about sets of stories that together tell a good story to the market. The iteration plan is synchronized to the rhythms of programming. Two weeks is long enough to

⬥ Develop some new functionality

⬥ Do a substantial refactoring

⬥ Develop some infrastructure

⬥ Try some experiments

⬥ Recover from little disappointments

Unlike the release plan, the iteration plan is very much the developers'. They decide how to do things and in what order. The customer is still involved. It's important to report progress mid-iteration so that the customer can see what's happening and get a sense for what will actually happen. The customer will also get involved if the team finds there is too much to do and you need to cut scope.

The formal start of the iteration is the iteration planning meeting, where the programmers get together to break down the stories for that iteration into tasks. We do this because we need smaller units to track than the stories. Each task is about one to three ideal days long. While it's often worthwhile to have a programmer responsible for seeing a story through to completion, it is better for people to sign up for the smaller tasks to give them a chance to express their specializations. Stories can share work, and we can handle this better by having them share tasks. Finally, the kind of dependencies that drive most planners crazy must be dealt with inside of iterations.

After the iteration planning meeting someone takes on the responsibility of tracking the iteration (Chapter 19). This person, the tracker, keeps an eye on which tasks are done and how much is left on outstanding tasks. Her job is to alert the team to problems that might come up: having too much to do, too little to do, people overcommitted or undercommitted. Every day the team has a short stand-up meeting so everyone can see what everyone else is doing. This helps keep communication flowing across the whole team.

Never Slip the Date

One of the most important principles in planning for Extreme Programming is that the dates are hard dates, but scope will vary. In every project you'll run into the situation where there is too much to do and you'll be tempted to slip the date of an iteration just a little bit to accommodate a little more functionality.

Don't do that.

Slipping dates is one of those bad habits that is both addictive and damaging. The damage really comes from the fact that it's so easy to do. At some point, however, you'll either slip so much that you'll lose all credibility (and the project, too), or you'll run into some date that's very painful to slip, like a release date. If slipping dates is the only thing people know how to do, then that's what will happen, and the pain is great.

The harder but surer way to cope with too much to do is to defer functionality. Because it's harder it's more important to practice doing it. Only if the team (and especially the customer) practices this for every iteration will everyone be ready to do this when the really important date comes along. The most important stories are the ones the customer decides he can live without for the moment. Those stories can save projects.

- -

Sometimes it may be better to slip a release date. That's the customer's decision. It will involve many issues outside the scope of project planning. Only if everyone has practiced deferring function will the customer have a genuine choice between date and function. We are constantly surprised by how much "essential" functionality customers can do without when a big date looms.

Often you can make those hard choices only when the big dates appear, and without practice you can't do it under pressure. As Jim Highsmith says, "I used to think time-boxing was about time, but I've learned that instead it is about forcing hard tradeoff decisions throughout the project."

The other reason not to slip dates is that you lose control. There's always some uncertainty within the iteration. Only at the end of an iteration do you really know where you are. So you never want to put that time off.

Chapter 18

Iteration Planning Meeting

At the beginning of an iteration the team creates an iteration plan. This plan breaks down the iteration into development tasks of a few days, each with a programmer responsible for its completion.

The iteration planning meeting is the first thing you do in the iteration. It shouldn't take any more than a day, and most teams will do it in under a day. All of the team should attend, as well as the customer. Find a comfortable room with plenty of whiteboard space.

Here's an overview of the sequence. (This is just a summary. We'll describe what it all means in a moment.)

- ✧ Read out the stories for this iteration.
- ✧ Write on the whiteboard all the tasks that need to be done for each story.
- ✧ Add to the list any technical tasks that need doing.
- ✧ Developers sign up and estimate tasks up to their individual velocity.
- ✧ If any story isn't completely signed up for, the customer is asked to defer some stories.
- ✧ If there is extra time, the customer is asked to add stories.

Understanding the Story

The first thing to do is to remind everyone what's on the menu for this iteration. It's often a good idea for the customer to read out the stories so that everyone hears them from the customer's perspective.

A short sentence on a card is enough to act as marker and reminder for a story. It certainly isn't enough to plan out a story, let alone write the code. So the customer needs to prepare for the iteration planning session by going into more detail about the stories. We've several ways of doing this.

- The simplest is for the customer to give a short talk about the story. This is simple and verbal and often works just fine
- The next simplest is for the customer to produce a written description of the details of the story. This is a few pages of corroborating detail. We call this a narrative. (As we go to press, Martin's current project has no narratives longer than four pages in the next iteration.)
- The most detailed approach is to provide a full set of acceptance tests for the story.

You'll need the acceptance tests eventually, so tests are the best format for corroborating detail. It seems to be impossible to get the acceptance tests at the beginning of the iteration. The narrative is a reasonable facsimile, providing that everyone understands that the narrative is a supplement to conversation not a substitute for it.

You'll need to find out what works best in your environment. Over the course of a few iterations you should find what works best for your team.

Listing the Tasks for an Iteration

Each story is a few ideal weeks of effort, so for this detail of planning we need to break the story down into a few finer-grained tasks. Each task should be a few ideal days of effort. The tasks are development tasks, so they don't need to make sense to the customer.

The best way to come up with the tasks is for everyone involved to just brainstorm what they might be. Often this will involve a little thought about how you're going to build the story. You don't need a major design effort here, but you do need just enough to get a good list of tasks. Take a short pass at the classes and interactions you'll need to add and modify. Remember that the goal is not to design everything that is needed for the iteration; it is to help figure what the best task breakdown is. You'll do other design sessions as part of carrying out the tasks.

Often you'll find overlap between the stories. This overlap may give you the opportunity to build software that helps satisfy several stories at once. There may be existing designs from past iterations that, with a little refactoring, could significantly help this iteration. Add tasks for this. It's great to have tasks that satisfy more than one story.

For example, several of the stories may require that as you enter text into a field you hunt for possible completions for that text from a given list. It would be a shame to develop this facility three or four times, once for each story. So make this into a task. It may be that other stories from past iterations need to have this new feature retrofitted onto them. You might make that retrofit a separate task.

You'll likely find dependencies between tasks. You won't need PERT charts or similar beasts. With a team that is communicating over a few weeks you can rely on the team to sort these dependencies out. It's worth talking them over, to influence what tasks are addressed first. However, as you'll see, you never plan precisely when each task gets done, or in what order the task gets done.

In the end there's no hard and fast rules for how you break something down into tasks. Use whatever approach makes sense for you. As long as the tasks are kept short and you can write tests for them, you'll be fine.

Technical Tasks

Most of your time will be spent in building stories. However, there are some purely technical tasks the customer doesn't care about but that still need to be done. These include installing the vendor's database upgrade, refactoring some messy bit of the system, trying out a design idea to learn if it will be useful, and improving the configuration control process. Anything like this should be added to the list. Again, it's important to keep each task small, so break the work into tasks of a few ideal days.

Ron Jeffries claims he can turn any technical task into a business-oriented story the customer can either schedule this iteration or not as she chooses. There's something to be said for not having any technical tasks. Once you start down the slippery slope of setting the priority for technical reasons, it's hard to stop. Dave Cleal suggests that a fixed portion of the budget, say 10 percent, be set aside for the programmers to spend as they like. We haven't tried it, but it sounds interesting.

Measuring the Velocity of a Programmer

How do you make sure individual programmers don't overcommit? During iteration planning there's pressure to be seen by the team to be doing your part. Fear of censure can overwhelm a programmer's experience.

We use Yesterday's Weather to reduce the chance of this happening regularly. Each programmer measures his velocity by tracking his accomplishments every iteration. A programmer can only sign up for the same number of days' worth of tasks as he completed last iteration.

There are good reasons to modify this number. If someone is spending one week of this three-week iteration on vacation, he will only have two-thirds of his velocity available.

A programmer's velocity is not a measure of productivity, speed, or goalkeeping ability. It just says how many tasks he can sign up for. One person may have a low velocity because he is naturally optimistic when estimating. Another may have a low velocity because he spends a lot of time helping other developers. It's more important for a programmer to make accurate predictions than for him to reach any arbitrary productivity measure. The absolute value of velocity is far less important than its predictive capability.

Signing Up and Estimating Tasks

Once you have a list of the tasks on the whiteboard, programmers can then start signing up for them. By signing up, a programmer accepts the responsibility for working on that task during the iteration. The first thing she needs to do is to estimate how long it will take her to do the task.

It's up to the programmer to decide how to come up with an estimate. As usual, the best approach is to compare a task with previous work. The programmer can say, "This should take about the same time as the shipping GUI I did last iteration." The project records will show how long that task took, so that number can be used this time.

Be wary of using comparable work from another programmer. We are dealing with people, not Plug Compatible Programming Units. Programmers do not work at the same speed, and their speed will be different for a task. It's useful to let a programmer look at the records to help come up with an estimate, but don't say, "It only took Dinsdale three days to do this task, so why do you think it'll take you five?" Once you start using the records as a club, you'll never get an honest estimate again. The most important thing here is to get estimates as accurately as you can—if you want to compare programmers' abilities, don't do it during planning.

Programmers should always assume they have a partner when doing a task, since in XP all production coding is done in pairs. It may be that a particular partner can affect the estimate. "If Spiny will work with me on this, we can do it in two days." That's fine. Indeed it reinforces the principle that people help each other.

Programmers should also assume that they aren't done with a task until they have all the unit tests written and passing. "I'm done with the coding, but I haven't tested it yet," is a meaningless statement in XP. Code without tests simply doesn't exist for planning purposes.

Programmers can sign up for whatever they want to do. People can work on things they have a desire to do, which keeps them motivated. Since motivation is the key to productivity, this is a Good Thing. Some programmers will pick one kind of task they prefer and mostly do this. Others like to broaden their interests by trying new things. This is a Good Thing because it keeps up motivation, it allows developers to grow their skills, and it reduces project risk.

In iteration planning, as indeed in all of this book, we've focused on what the programmers do. How about the tasks others need to do: writing documentation, designing icons, and so on? In iteration planning we've seen some success from breaking down the work into tasks and just adding them to the list. Technical writers then sign up for the user manuals and artists sign up for icon design at the same time programmers sign up for programming.

Scut Work

Some project managers on hearing about this "signing up" practice fear there'll be some dirty work that doesn't get done. In practice we don't find this is an issue. Developers are so varied that there is almost always someone who likes doing anything. For occasional unpopular tasks, some informal and often unspoken sharing goes on.

If someone always ends up with the short end of the stick, ask the team to come up with a solution. Team members may choose to do a more formal rotation to take turns doing unpopular work. They may try to recruit someone to the team who likes doing this kind of work. Programmers like solving problems, so they'll find a solution. If they come up with the solution, they will work to make it fly.

Too Much to Do

Once all the programmers have signed up for tasks and estimated them, take a look at your task list. In a perfect world all the tasks will be signed up for. In this particular galaxy, we often find that some tasks remain unclaimed. If you have orphan tasks, which tasks do you defer?

Can you wait another iteration to upgrade the database? Sometimes waiting is the best option, but other times there aren't any technical tasks you think you can defer.

If no technical tasks can be defered, ask the customer. "We are short five ideal days. We need you to remove five ideal days' worth of story."

Customers can defer a whole story, or they can choose to split a story and defer one of the resulting parts (see "Splitting User Stories" on page 49). A customer may choose to split several stories to get the right mix. A deferred story goes on the list for the next iteration. The customer can consider it again in two weeks.

You may be tempted to adjust the whole release plan if you defer a story. Don't rush to do that. Go for an iteration or two before you rework the release plan. Often the deferments are too small to be an issue right away. They need to build up before it's worth trying to deal with them.

Too Little to Do

Go ahead, laugh, but it does happen from time to time.

This process is the reverse of too much to do. The programmers ask the customer to add some stories. The customer can add a whole story or split a story and move a part in. However, as usual, the customer decides what gets moved, not the programmers.

Iteration Plan

We'll dig some more stuff out of the time capsule to show the iteration plan for the second iteration. The notes look like this:

Find lowest fare.

Alternative fare finder object—KB 2

Find candidate fares by date range—MF 1

Update planet ports to find alternatives—KB 1

Find candidate fares for alternative ports—KB 1

Special offers—major space lines—MF 2

Special offers—low-price space lines—RJ 3

UI for low fares—RJ 1

Review itineraries.

Simple UI display of itineraries—WC 2

Display detail for one itinerary—RJ 2

Book a hotel.

Hotel booking interfacer—MF 1

Interface to IHAB—MF 2

Interface to HiHat—MF 1

Interface to Mary's Rote—MF 1

Interface to HillTown—WC 1

Interface to Best Southern—RJ 1

Interface to Woodstar—WC 1

(Show hotels—IHAB by city.)

Query IHAB for hotels for named city—WC 2

UI for named city display—WC 1

Other

UI cleanup—KA 2

Network performance improvement—KB 2

Investigate using IPv84—KB 1

Notes:

- ✧ The tasks in the stories don't necessarily add up to the estimates in the release plan. "Book a hotel" was marked as one ideal week but comes out as eight ideal days. "Find lowest fare" was three ideal weeks but came out as eleven ideal days. This is quite usual as you start estimating in more detail and have more information about the iteration. In this case they cancel out pretty well, but they may not. That's why we don't write down the original story estimate in the iteration plan. Otherwise, we will be tempted to force fit the task estimates to sum to the story estimate. Then we would be planning with lower-quality information. If the task estimates say you are overcommitted, go back to the customer.

- ✧ Because there is time left over, the team took "Show hotels" and built a little piece of it. Here the customer split "Show hotels" to get a piece that was useful and enough for the team to use up the extra time it had available.

- ✧ Most team members have a velocity of seven. KA has a velocity of two. Maybe he's part-time or new to the team or just estimates differently.

- ✧ There are plenty of dependencies in the tasks, but the plan doesn't note any of them. From watching the videos we could tell that the alternative fare finder object was needed before you could find candidate fares by date range or find candidate fares for alternative ports. Also, you need to do the update of planet ports to show alternatives before you can find candidates for alternative ports. None of this is on the plan. Because this is an XP team we can safely assume that MF and KB are intelligent beings who will communicate about the order in which things need to be done and will sort things out between them.

Chapter 19

Tracking an Iteration

A couple of times a week, the tracker checks progress on the iteration to see how things are going.

You have an iteration plan, so now all you have to do is sit back and watch the plan unfold—right? If you said yes, hit yourself on the head three times with this book (and be glad it's a thin one).

The only thing you know about a plan is that things won't go according to it. So you have to monitor the iteration at regular intervals. You need to have someone whose job it is to track progress in an iteration. We call this person the tracker.

Iteration Progress Check

A couple of times a week or so the tracker needs to find out where everyone is with the iteration. We don't suggest calling a meeting for this or (heaven forbid) writing a report. Instead, the tracker should visit each programmer one at a time.

The tracker asks developers two questions about each task they signed up for:

⬦ How many ideal days have you worked on this?
⬦ How many more ideal days do you need before you're done?

Notice we don't ask for the percentage complete. We've found that such a question generates a nearly meaningless answer. To monitor how much work there is left, the key question is how many days are left.

(Knowing how much has been done so far is more important for building the historic record.)

At this point you can add up the figures for all the programmer's tasks and assess the situation.

Most important is what is left to do. How does the amount of ideal days of effort compare with the developer's remaining calendar time? This comparison is always somewhat rough. There's no point using a ratio of the remaining calendar time because the developer won't get to work ideal days evenly through the iteration. But if there is a big difference, that's a warning sign. It's also definitely a warning sign if there are more ideal days of things to do than calendar days left to do them.

To a large extent the analysis is up to the programmer. Does she think she has too much to do? The tracker's role is to ask simple questions and point out possible problems. In the end it is the programmer's judgement whether she will be able to get in enough ideal days before the end of the iteration.

At this stage you don't do much with the "How many days so far" question. Primarily that's to help you get a list of tasks done with how many ideal days they actually took. Asking each time is better than asking at the end of the iteration when nobody can remember how much time they spent on anything last week.

A very important part of this process is the fact that the tracker should personally talk to each programmer about status. You get so much information from physical cues and gut feel. The figures are valuable. Just as important is the sense of how the programmer feels about progress, which takes into account both the state of the task and the personality of the programmer. The personal touch is essential to the tracker's job of monitoring progress.

One thing to watch is if a programmer reports a lot less ideal time spent on tasks than usual. This might mean nothing—she was just doing a lot of helping this week—or it may mean there's something else that's chewing up her time. Perhaps the programmer needs some help clearing the decks.

Take the old figures to the programmer. That way you are asking only for the change since the last progress check. But don't take the original estimates. You want to avoid any tendency to make the new estimates match the old ones.

Getting Closure

Rob Mee and Edward Hiatt

Coached by Rob Mee, and with frequent input from Kent Beck, we as an XP team knew from the start of our project the importance of constant collaboration between customers and developers. In particular, we set aside a day or more at the start of each three-week iteration when the programmers and the customers huddled together hammering out the features and tasks that had been scheduled for that time period. After this kick-off day the tasks were written on posters and hung up on the wall, waiting to be ticked off as they were completed. Throughout the iteration programmers asked the customers for clarification of requirements; at the same time, customers nudged the emerging product this way and that as they saw what they had imagined taking shape. When a pair of developers completed a task, they went to the wall poster and crossed it off, and moved on to the next one.

Ideal as that might sound, there was a problem. Notice how the developers weren't crossing off tasks when they were done. They were crossing them off when they *thought* they were done. The collaboration hadn't been taken far enough. In spite of the close cooperation during development, the programmers were taking that final step, that *business decision*, by themselves. This had unpleasant consequences. After the task had been crossed off, the customers would look at the feature and say, "That doesn't work quite right. It needs a minor adjustment." With the process unclear about how to go back in a situation like this, the customers would simply log the discrepancy as a bug.

As time went by, the bug list grew: incompletions, small deficiencies, and simple misunderstandings were being added to the bug list. Management started pressuring the developers to lower the bug count. Developers resented the pressure because many of the items clearly weren't "bugs"; they were just clarifications or even changes of mind. Customers resented having the overhead of the extra tracking. Everybody knew the root of the problem was a communication issue, not a lack of competency. But how to fix it? We were already in constant communication.

Finally the project manager, Vraj Mohan, saw the simple solution: It should be the customer, not the developer, who would cross off tasks at completion. This would force the final collaborative step that had been missing from the process. Once this step was instituted, most of the friction that had been developing melted away. Programmers had a much more confident sense of completion—if the customer saw the final piece of work and was satisfied, the developers could be sure that they were finished with the task. Customers still wanted changes in features after completion, but now the changes were viewed as enhancements or additional features that they themselves had generated, rather than as bugs that were the fault of the programmers.

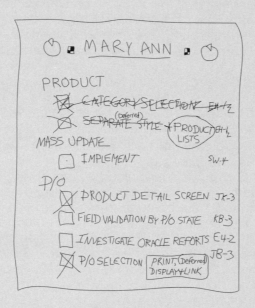

Sharing the Glory

At the end of each iteration, the whole team would gather round and watch the developers demo the work in which each had been involved in the preceding three weeks. This was partly so that everyone could be kept abreast of the latest developments, and partly as a morale boost—it's gratifying for the developer-customer team to show off the work they have done together to the rest of the team. We would walk down the task list, and for each crossed-off task, one of the developers from the pair that had worked on the task would step forward and demo the feature.

As each task came up to be demoed, there was often a hesitation as the two developers who had paired on the task decided on who would be the one to demo the feature. At one such point, at the end of the third or fourth iteration, there happened to be a long delay. To end the wait, the customer whose feature it was stepped forward and good-naturedly announced that she herself would demo it instead of waiting for the developers to decide. It was done on the spur of the moment and brought a laugh from the team watching on; but as Rob and Kent thought about what had just happened, they realized that this was an excellent idea. Why not always have customers demo their features? It would ensure without a doubt that customers would keep up with the work being done during the iteration. In front of an audience, everyone wants to be prepared for their "performance," so no customers would want to lose track of what progress had been made on their features.

This process has become popular. It encourages the customer to keep in closer contact with the developer pair: We have found that customers are more eager to check in with developers to see new work as soon as possible, which tends to lead to closer matching of the customer's vision with the final product.

Falling Behind

Tracking is passive, until you find that something is up. Up in this case means the programmer realizes she can't complete all the tasks she signed up for. There are plenty of reasons this can happen, but the most important point is to do something about it.

The first reaction is to look for someone else with time available who is willing to accept the task. He should then give his own estimate of how much time is needed to finish the task. If his estimate ends up greater than the time available, the problem hasn't been solved yet.

If nobody has enough time to take on the task, then the team needs to figure out what to do about it. It's important to let everyone know about the problem, as someone may have a good solution at hand. This is where the stand-up meeting comes in handy. Often a bit of informal juggling of a couple people's time can overcome the problem.

If there aren't any great solutions available, you have to go to the customer and tell her the score. The customer will need to know what work has been completed on what stories. She then goes through much the same process as she did at the beginning of the iteration: choose a story to defer or split a story and defer a part. The sooner you bring the situation to the customer's attention, the more options she has for salvaging the greatest possible business value out of the iteration.

It's annoying for the customer to do this in the middle of the iteration, so the team should work to avoid this. The key cure to this problem is to get better at estimating, and this can only come with practice and good task records. Over time mid-iteration corrections should happen less often. If they aren't occurring less often, the team needs to figure out what is going wrong. While the story estimates are pretty vague, once you get down to tasks in the iteration plan, you shouldn't get such big swings.

We've heard this line from project managers: "XP is an excuse for my programmers to tell me I can't have what I want." Customers aren't ever happy about having to cut already-committed scope. Sometimes customers can't have what they want. Who is going to decide what they don't get—the customers, the programmers, the project managers, or chance?

What about overtime? The simple rule is that no one can work overtime two weeks in a row. If someone wants to crank for a day or two to get caught up, fine. But then don't expect full results from that person for a day or two.

When a Programmer Has Extra Time

Inevitably this is the least frequent but also the more pleasant problem. The first choice is to look at other people's task load and see if the programmer can help others. Often you'll have a mix on the team that balances out.

If not, then it's off to the customer again to see what can be brought forward, either a full story or part of a story.

But if the programmer has had a heavy load in recent iterations, consider letting him take a break. This may mean a day off if he has had to use overtime recently. It may mean some time experimenting—spending a day looking at some bit of technology that might be useful. Such breaks help keep people motivated and may lead to useful ideas that'll help the project.

When Is the Iteration Done?

The iteration is done on the date that was set at the beginning. A two-week iteration ends in two weeks, no buts. Stories that are done, are done. Stories that are not done are deferred to be considered for implementation in the next iteration planning meeting.

When Is a Story Done?

A story is done when the function of that story is demonstated to the customer and the customer agrees that the functionality substantially fulfills what is expected.

What do we mean by the weasel words "substantially fulfills"? The customer is paying the tab, so the customer decides if she is satisfied.

The customer should run the acceptance tests for that story. There may be failures. The customer then decides whether the failures are enough to warrant saying that the story isn't done. If the charges on the phone bill print out wrong, then the customer will probably say, "No, the story isn't acceptable." If the formatting is one pica off, she may say, "Okay, there are bugs, but we'll take the software." Plenty of people ship software with known bugs. Some ship software with plenty of known bugs. As long as the customer knows the score, it's up to her what she will accept.

Example Iteration Tracking

Back into the time capsule to look at some iteration tracking done two-thirds of the way through the second iteration. You can show the state of the iteration with a simple table.

Table 19.1 gives us the state of the iteration. The bottom line warns us of potential problems. KA is gone until the end of the iteration, so we have four people. We plan that each can do 7 ideal days in a three-week iteration. The four people can do 28 ideal days in the whole iteration. In the last week, they can do roughly a third of that: 9 days. But we have 14 days of work to go.

Looking at the tasks and individual states we can see some more details. RJ is pretty much on track, with three ideal days to go. Talking to him brings out that he is comfortable that he will complete his work on time.

TABLE 19.1 Tasks at the End of the Third Week

Task	Who	Done	To Do
UI cleanup	KA	2	0
KA Total (out till end)		2	0
Alternative fare finder object	KB	2	0
Update planet ports to find alternatives	KB	1	1
Find candidate fares for alternative ports	KB	0	1
Network performance improvement	KB	2	2
Investigate using IPv84	KB	0	1
KB Total		5	5
Special offers—major space lines	MF	0	2
Find candidate fares by date range	MF	0	1
Hotel booking interfacer	MF	1	0
Interface to IHAB	MF	3	2
Interface to HiHat	MF	1	0
Interface to Mary's Rote	MF	0	1
MF Total		5	6
Special offers—budget space lines	RJ	2	1
UI for low fares	RJ	0	1
Display detail for one itinerary	RJ	2	0
Interface to Best Southern	RJ	0	1
RJ Total		4	3
Simple UI display of itineraries	WC	1	0
Interface to HillTown	WC	0.5	0
Interface to Woodstar	WC	0.5	0
Query IHAB for hotels for named city	WC	2	0
UI for named city display	WC	0.5	0
WC Total		4.5	0
Team Total		20.5	14

WC is very comfortable. His tasks worked out easier than he thought. He is free for the last week.

However, both KB and MF are in trouble with a quite a bit of outstanding time. We can do a bit of shuffling here by bringing in WC, but it won't be enough. So we need to talk to the customer to decide what

TABLE 19.2 Work Remaining on Stories

Story	To Do	Comments
Find lowest fare	7	Several pieces incomplete
Review Itineraries	0	
Book a hotel	4	IHAB interface a problem; can pick and choose with others
Show hotels (IHAB by city)	0	
Other	3	Mainly performance work

needs to be done. The customer can look at the tasks, but primarily he looks at the state of the stories.

The customer knows we have around nine ideal days available. What should be cut? "Find lowest fare" is the key story here. It needs to be done at all costs. "Book a hotel" is less important and the performance work is not that critical to the customer; otherwise it would be a story. So this allows the team to look at the tasks afresh and sign up again for the ones that need work. Table 19.3 shows the outstanding tasks.

TABLE 19.3 Tasks for the Last Week

Outstanding Task	Who	To Do
Update planet ports to find alternatives	KB	1
Find candidate fares for alternative ports	KB	1
~~Network Performance Improvement~~	~~KB~~	~~2~~
~~Investigate using IPv84~~	~~KB~~	~~1~~
KB Total		2
Find candidate fares by date range	MF	1
~~Interface to IHAB~~	~~MF~~	~~2~~
Interface to Mary's Rote	MF	1
MF Total		2
Special offers—low-price space lines	RJ	1
UI for low fares	RJ	1
Interface to Best Southern	RJ	1
RJ Total		3
Special offers—major space lines	WC	2
WC Total		2

The new plan defers further performance improvement. To focus on the lowest price story, WC picks up the special offers task from MF. The customer says that he would rather get the Mary's Rote interface than the problematic IHAB interface, so MF drops the latter completely.

(The format of the task tables is just one way to track tasks. Every team of ours has come up with its own format.)

Chapter 20

Stand-up Meetings

When a meeting gets boring, leave.
—Robert Cecil "Uncle Bob" Martin

Have a short meeting once a day so everybody knows what's going on, and what's not.

You'll notice we aren't into lots of meetings. Meetings are at the top of most programmers' lists of boring time wasters. But meetings are also a way for people to communicate. The challenge is to figure out what kind of meetings work well.

We've found that short daily meetings are invaluable for giving everyone an idea of what other people are doing. However the emphasis is on short. If the daily meetings ever start dragging, you'll run into trouble.

The stand-up meeting gets its name from one of the tricks we use to keep it short: Everyone has to stand up for the whole meeting. That reminds everyone to be brief. If they don't remember, remind them again (with a stick if necessary).

The format is simple. Everyone stands in a circle and you go round person by person (whether you go with or against the clock is up to you). Each person briefly says what he or she did yesterday and what he or she is doing today. Problems or announcements that are important to the team are passed on.

The purpose of the stand-up is to communicate problems, not to solve them. Keep the meeting brief. The usual stumbling block is when somebody says, "I implemented some code to the floop the foobar," someone else says, "I did something like that last month," "Oh, I needed a triple axel," "You can do that by modifying the config file." Suddenly it's on the way to being a long conversation. At this point you suggest, "Maybe you should get together this morning and talk about this." Anything that requires anything more than a brief announcement should be shunted off to another session where only those who are interested need to attend.

Have the stand-up meeting daily, so everyone knows roughly what everyone's doing. Pick the same time every day, and aim at a time when everyone is there. Earlier in the day is better, as that allows time for people to get together quickly if they need to.

Chapter 21

Visible Graphs

Anyone should be able to sense the state of the project by looking
at a handful of graphs in the team's working area.

We are big fans of the scientific method. Emotional outbursts like,
"I think you are going too slow," or, "This software is riddled with
bugs," don't help when you're trying to steer a software project. How
fast are we going? What variety of Swiss cheese does the software most
closely resemble?

Deming says, "You can't manage what you can't measure." We're
sure this isn't true, because lots of software gets shipped without any
metrics being gathered. However, if you choose to manage without
metrics, you are committing yourself to a degree of emotional detach-
ment that is difficult to maintain, especially under pressure. The numbers help you look your fears in the face. Once you've acknowledged
your fear you can use informed intuition to make your decision.

The danger with a "scientific" approach to planning is that the measurements can become the end instead of the means. The overhead of
data collection can swamp real work. The process can become inhu-
mane, with people—messy, smelly, distractable, inspired, unpredictable
people—conveniently abstracted away to a set of numbers.

That's not what we are talking about. Don't do that.

Instead, here is a process that combines intuition and measurement:

1. Smell a problem.
2. Devise a measurement.

3. Display the measurement.

4. If the problem doesn't go away, return to 2.

Examples

Here are some examples from a real XP project that has been operating for ten iterations. The team devised an ingenious low-cost data-gathering technique. First, the team is small enough (five programmers) that team members don't need to distinguish between stories and tasks. Their stories are small, between four and twenty hours. On the back of each story card is a little table:

Pair		*Date*	*Hours*
——	——	———	——
——	——	———	——
——	——	———	——
——	——	———	——
——	——	———	——

At the end of every iteration, someone types in all the values on the backs of the cards onto a spreadsheet. The raw data can then be presented in many different forms.

Productivity

Team members began to get the feeling that they were going slower than they should. Rather than do something obviously ineffective like work longer hours, they decided to measure. The measure they chose was the percentage of office hours spent on programming.

It's obvious from Figure 21.1 that the team just wasn't spending many hours programming. No wonder it was going slowly. A little reflection showed that the hours dropped about the time the team

   ✧ Split to start a second project, and
   ✧ Acquired external customers

No wonder the team didn't have as much time for programming. After doing what they could to increase programming time, team members modified their release plan to reflect their new measured velocity.

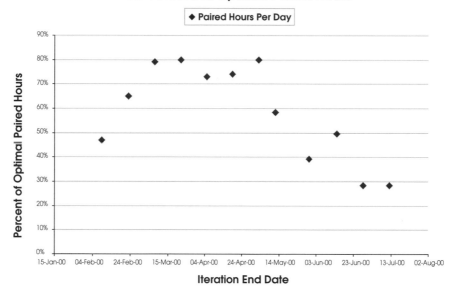

FIGURE 21.1 Measured Overhead

Integration Hell (Well, "Heck" Anyway)

Another problem that began to smell was that integrations were taking too long and were the source of too many errors. The team started tracking how long they were programming together before integrating (see Figure 21.2).

The trend toward longer and longer programming sessions was obvious. The consequence was that people were exhausted when they finally integrated, increasing the probability of errors. Also, the delay before integrating increased the probability of conflicts with the changes from other pairs. Once the measurement was in place (on June 14), the average duration of a pairing session dropped to two hours and integration got easier.

This example illustrates an important principle of management by measurement: indirection. The team could have separately started tracking how long each integration took and tried to optimize integration. By finding the root cause of difficult integrations, team members were able to treat the cause, not just the symptoms.

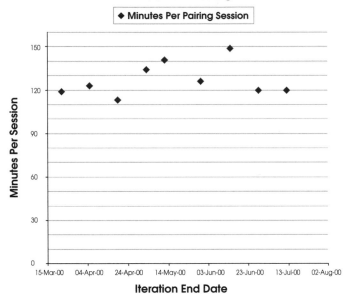

FIGURE 21.2 Longer Sessions Slow Integration

Choosing Which Graphs to Show

Here are some graphs you may want to use. Choose your graphs carefully. Consider what things you, your management, your programmers, and the customers are concerned about. For each worry try to think of a simple graph that'll demonstrate what's happening to everyone present.

When a graph has done its job, drop it. Graphs are a powerful tool, but too many of them blunts their purpose. Everyone should know that the graphs count, and the chore of plotting them should be compensated by the warm feelings about the useful information you are gaining.

Many people suggest putting these graphs on a Web site. This is good if people on remote sites need to see what's happening. But don't let that be a substitute for putting them on the wall in the developers' area. Web sites don't get looked at if they aren't clicked on. You can't avoid what's on the bathroom wall. Many an insight comes when idly staring at a graph when you're half doing something else.

Here are a handful of graphs we've been glad we used:

- ✧ Acceptance Tests Defined and Passing
- ✧ Production Code Bulk versus Test Code Bulk
- ✧ Integrations
- ✧ Bug Density
- ✧ Story Progress
- ✧ System Performance

The most important thing to remember is to *select the graphs you need and stop producing graphs you don't*. Although we'll be flattered if you pick the graphs we suggest, it's far more important that you think about your worries and choose graphs that illustrate your worries. Just trying to figure out what the graphs should be will probably do a lot to help you think through your issues. After all, we already get enough flattery.

Chapter 22

Dealing with Bugs

This is for the species, boys and girls.
—Starship Troopers

Schedule bug fixes with stories so the customer can choose between fixing bugs and adding further functionality.

We've never tried farming, even though Kent now lives in the middle of farms, pick-up trucks, and people who wear cowboy hats for real. One thing we imagine we have in common with farmers is a distaste for bugs. Programming bugs may not eat our source code, but they do eat at our customer relationships and productivity. And we can't get software insecticide at the nearest supply shop.

Why are we even talking about bugs? Don't XP's testing practices lead to defect-free systems? No. There should be far fewer defects, but there will still be some. There may even be enough to need managing.

One of the worst things about software bugs is that they come with a strong element of blame (from the customer) and guilt (from the programmer). If only we'd tested more, if only you were competent programmers, there wouldn't be these bugs. We've seen people screaming on news groups and managers banging on tables saying that no bugs are acceptable. All this emotion really screws up the process of dealing with bugs and hurts the key human relationships that are essential if software development is to work well.

So let's get a few ground rules on the table.

We assume that the programmers are trying to do the most professional job they can. As part of this they will go to great lengths to eliminate bugs. But nobody can eliminate all of them. The customer has to trust that the programmers are working hard to reduce bugs, and can monitor the testing process to see that they are doing as much as they should.

For most software, however, we don't actually want zero bugs. (Now there's a statement that we guarantee will be used against us out of context.) Any defect, once it's in there, takes time and effort to remove. That time and effort will take away from effort spent putting in features. So you have to decide which to do. Even when you know about a bug, someone has to decide whether you want to eliminate the bug or add another feature. Who decides? In our view it must be the customer. The customer has to make a business decision based on the cost of having the bug versus the value of having another feature—or the value of deploying now instead of waiting to reduce the bug count.

(We would argue that this does not hold true for bugs that could be life-threatening. In that case we think the programmers have a duty to public safety that is far greater than their duty to the customer.)

There are plenty of cases where the business decision is to have the feature instead. Perhaps some readers can think of a software product they use regularly that they think has more bugs than it should. The company made a business decision to add features rather than fix bugs. Look at their share price over the last few years to determine if that was a good choice.

We once ran into a sharp example of this. We were involved in a project to replace an existing system. The customer decided to delay deployment because of bugs that, despite the team's best efforts, were still there. It then transpired that during one month the existing system, due to its bugs, lost the company several million dollars. The new bugs weren't anywhere near that expensive. Was the customer right to delay deployment? In hindsight we think not, although we agreed with the decision at the time.

Dealing with Production Defects

The most important thing is to remove the emotion. A bug report is a request for a change to the deployed system. Many of these changes could be considered to be enhancements rather than defect fixes. We don't encourage you to try to classify them one way or the other, because doing so usually leads to unhelpful finger pointing.

First determine if the bug is critical. To do this and to deal with it see Dealing with Critical Bugs below.

If it's not critical, then log it on a card. Get development to look at it and estimate the effort involved to eliminate it. A lot of the time you don't know what's involved at this stage so mark it as unknown. If it's less than an ideal day mark it as small.

If the estimate is more than a day's worth of effort, treat the defect as a story. The customer can then say which iteration should address the defect, just as with any other story. Usually it's worth lumping several bugs together to get a week's worth.

Just before the next iteration planning meeting the customer should take the small and unknown bugs and prioritize them. The customer should indicate how much ideal time the developers should spend dealing with them. "Squash little bugs" becomes a story that goes into the iteration planning exercise.

We want to encourage everyone to deal with bugs in a rational way, to make sensible tradeoffs between fixing defects and adding features. No two projects have the same priorities here. If fixing bugs in an absolute must, then you do them first using this process.

At this point we have to declare a health warning. We haven't managed to try this pure a process in action. Instead we've seen people use a production support team.

Production Support Team

Two or four programmers volunteer to focus on fixing bugs. Each programmer spends a couple of iterations in production support, then rotates back to development. In every iteration there is at least one developer doing his first iteration of support and at least one doing her second. Someone always has the responsibility for production support, and this (occasionally unpleasant) work is rotated around the team.

This has worked fairly well. But the customer didn't fully appreciate what he was trading off to get production support. Production support became overhead, a separate lump of effort that was scheduled independently of the rest of development. As such the customer wasn't forced to go through the explicit tradeoffs that he had to undergo elsewhere.

Dealing with Critical Bugs

There are some bugs that can't wait until the next iteration. They really do have to be fixed now, or at least this week. The difficulty is identifying which things really are critical bugs. Only the customer can make this call. Remove the emotion if you can and follow a similar process to the standard one: Programmers estimate how long it will take to fix, customer sets priorities. Programmers may well have no idea how long the fix will take, in which case they'd better investigate. Then the customer picks which story on the current plan takes the hit. That way the customer is explicitly making a tradeoff of function (or even other bug fixes) versus fixing this bug. (People make this tradeoff implicitly all the time. We prefer things to be explicit.)

Chapter 23

Changes to the Team

When the team changes, how does that affect your planning?

Coming

Give new team members an iteration or two to get acclimated. They can

⋄ Pair with more experienced folks

⋄ Read code and test cases

⋄ Talk to customers

During this orientation, we haven't found the need to predict a reduction in the team's velocity. Time spent answering newbie questions is made up for in the new perspective they bring to old problems.

Yesterday's Weather will tell you when to increase your estimates based on the presence of new people. A project of Kent's added two new people to a team of eight and had a disastrous iteration, mostly because of deferred refactorings that caught up with them. The team declared that the "Lost Iteration" and planned for the next iteration as if the Lost Iteration hadn't happened. The next iteration they committed to 22 days of stories and completed 37. Was it the refactorings or the new folks? Impossible to tell, but the team was on a new, higher trajectory that has since been sustained.

Going

If you have five programmers and one leaves, reduce your next iteration by 20 percent. Yesterday's Weather will fix the new velocity quickly enough.

Splitting the Team

Ward Cunningham speculates that the way to scale XP up to 30 to 40 programmers is to complete the first release with a team of ten, then split into two teams. Each team gets its own stream of stories from its own customer. The teams of five then grow to ten. Do this twice and you're at 40.

For planning purposes, if we were to do this, we would begin committing each subteam to half of what the whole team accomplished before the split. Yesterday's Weather will quickly tell you how much cross-team overhead to plan for.

People Growing

People are different day to day. Testers become programmers, programmers become managers, managers throw off the shackles of oppression and become programmers again (oops, our bias is showing).

XP isn't executed by Plug Compatible Programming Units. It is executed by people, changing people. What if someone got bored with programming all the time? How could the team gracefully adapt to changes in lifestyle?

This is just an idea, but what if you put the management tasks on the board alongside the technical tasks during iteration planning? The project manager would typically sign up for tracking, the status report, and pizza selection. However, if someone else wanted to get a taste of project management, he could sign up for one from time to time. If the project manager needed to move on, someone could easily step in, even if only temporarily. The project manager could also take a programming task from time to time to see how things looked from ground level.

Chapter 24

Tools

(The French Marshals) planned their campaigns just as you might make a splendid set of harness. It looks very well, and answers very well, until it gets broken; and then you are done for. Now, I made my campaigns of ropes. If anything went wrong, I tied a knot; and went on.
—The Duke of Wellington

Stick with simple tools, like pencil, paper, and whiteboard. Communication is more important to success than whizbang.

There are two problems to solve in project management:

✧ Keeping track of all data
✧ Maintaining communication and relationships between people

Our tool strategy for project management is biased heavily towards maintaining human communication and the relationships between people. For small to medium-sized projects, keeping everybody talking honestly is a much more difficult problem to solve than calculating the schedule impact of surprises, so it deserves stronger tools. And the winner is: *little pieces of paper.*

The primary physical unit of schedule information on XP projects is the index card. Index cards are

✧ Portable
✧ Machine independent
✧ Approachable

♦ Cheap (sorry about this one—you can send us a bunch of money if you'd like, and we'll get Bob Martin to send you *really* nice index cards)

Remember our purposes in planning:

♦ Decide whether to go ahead
♦ Coordinate within the team and with the outside world
♦ Gauge the impact of surprises
♦ Set priorities

None of these are computationally impressive tasks. We can do the arithmetic in our heads and write the answers down on the cards. More complicated calculations can easily be handled by a spreadsheet. From this spreadsheet you can also generate all kinds of cool and impressive reports and graphs, some of which are even useful.

If you must use a spreadsheet, never forget that the spreadsheet is not as important as communication and relationships. "I discovered a couple more tasks for this iteration, but I don't want to edit all those reports." Time out! The tail is wagging the dog. Making sure everyone understands all the tasks required for this iteration is far more important than getting the reports exactly right this instant. If necessary, abandon the spreadsheet. If everyone understands but the spreadsheet is hopelessly out of date, that is much better than having a perfect record of incorrect information.

Chapter 25

Business Contracts

Traditional business relationships require a little tweaking if you're going to plan and execute a project with XP.

We know we promised to only talk about project planning, but the very best software development process in the world is helpless in the face of the wrong contract. Here we will talk briefly about three typical software businesses and how XP planning changes them:

⬧ Outsourcing
⬧ In-house development
⬧ Shrink-wrap

Any contract that pits the interests of the supplier against the interests of the customer is trouble. If the opposition becomes worse as pressure increases, the trouble is well nigh insurmountable.

Outsourcing

The typical outsourcing contract fixes three of the four variables:[1]

⬧ Scope
⬧ Time
⬧ Cost

---

1. Thanks to Dave Cleal for many of the refinements on negotiable scope contracts.

Unfortunately, it is impossible to fix all four variables. If there is a surprise, one of the variables will change (hence the name "variable"). Since quality is the hardest variable to measure, surprises tend to get absorbed by reducing quality—a little less testing, a little less design, a little less communication. Any attempt to rescue a plan by adding risk is doomed. Once you have an unknown amount of work lurking, scope, time, and cost will all explode.

The fundamental problem with fixed-scope contracts is that they pit the interests of supplier and customer directly against each other. Customers want as much scope as possible for their money, but suppliers want to do as little work as possible for the money. As long as everything is going according to plan, this opposition isn't necessarily fatal. When the surprises start adding up, the contract goes sour.

Instead, the contract could read, "Supplier will have eight programmers work for Customer for two months for $320,000. Scope will be negotiated every two weeks according to the classic book *Planning Extreme Programming*." That's it. Simple to write, simple to read (and it boosts our book sales).

But wait. The customer wants to know what she is going to get for her three hundred grand. Sure, she wants to know, but she can't know. Planning is not about predicting the future. We can give her the Big Plan. She can see our progress every two weeks. After all, it's only two months, and the project is likely to last for six to eight months. It's not likely you will send in scrubs and leave three-fourths of the money on the table.

But wait. The supplier wants to know what his employment requirements are for the next six months. Well, then, keep the customer as happy as you can.

In-House Development

In-house development has its own sets of advantages and disadvantages for XP. The advantages are

- ⬦ You don't have an explicit contract, so you don't have to worry about being sued if you fail—you may be fired, perhaps, but not sued. Okay, so this isn't such a big advantage.
- ⬦ You are working inside the same culture. Business and development are likely to share some values and myths (even if the roles of Good Guys and Bad Guys are reversed in some of the stories).

✧ You have a built-in arbitrator in "the big boss." Of course, you'd rather resolve your disagreements before they escalate that far, but at least there is a clear place where the buck stops.

The disadvantages are

✧ Business and development already have a history, and it is likely to be, well, a bit strained (if business and development get along swimmingly, you don't need XP, XP needs you).
✧ You likely have several customers to serve, not just one. Resolving conflicting priorities can take up all your energy.

The biggest problem with in-house projects is finding the customer. The best customer Kent ever saw was on a customer service system project. The customer had spent seven years opening envelopes and answering phones while using the legacy system. Then she spent three years supervising other representatives. This left her with complete knowledge of the existing system and an understanding of where the system was weak, where mistakes were likely to be made, where duplicate information was required. She was also fearless in making decisions but conscientious about verifying them after she made them.

It's best if you can find a single person who can confidently speak for business. This person needs

✧ Experience
✧ Contacts
✧ Vision
✧ Courage

If you can't find a single person to act as customer, you will have to have a committee of customers. Make this committee explicit. Insist that they get together to discuss your priorities. We watched a team go from corporate heroes to goats in one year because two customers had widely differing priorities. They were never explicit about their differences, and they did nothing to resolve them.

If the customers can't collaborate to decide on stories for releases and iterations, try an idea from Dave Cleal: Give each customer a budget. Let's say you've measured that your team can produce eight ideal weeks' worth of stories every iteration. Give the trading floor three weeks to spend and give the back office three weeks. Both customers will have to be present at every release planning meeting and each iteration planning meeting, and both will have to be available for answering questions throughout development.

Shrink-Wrap

How do you plan when you don't have one customer, you have hundreds, thousands, millions and billions and trillions of customers? XP requires the customer to speak with one voice.

This role is called "product manager" in most places. The product manager listens to many sources:

- ✧ Sales
- ✧ Marketing
- ✧ Customer support
- ✧ Customers

The product manager merges the stories, gets estimates from development, sets relative task priorities, and speaks to development through iteration and release planning. The key point is that responsibility for resolving conflicts is shifted away from development. If you can only satisfy two of three customers immediately, the product manager decides which two get stroked now and which one will be upset for a while.

Kent has a project where there are six product managers. One acts as the overall product manager, while the other five each have responsibility for a part of the product. Through some magic process completely invisible to development, they work out their relative priority iteration by iteration. By the time they get to the planning meeting, they present their stories with one voice.

Chapter 26

Red Flags

Here are some dicey situations we've seen more than once and what we wished we'd done about them.

Kent has a rolling suitcase whose wheels are too close together. When he is running between planes, the suitcase starts wobbling. Trying to hold on tighter to the handle just makes it wobble more. Eventually the stupid thing just falls over.

The solution, of course, is to buy a new suitcase with suitably spaced wheels. That wouldn't make much of a teaching story, though. Kent's solution is to slow down until the suitcase stops wobbling. It doesn't matter how late you are for your plane, if the suitcase falls over you'll be later.

Here are some common "wobbles," signs of trouble with planning, and what we do if we see them. The solutions are all some form of "slow down until you are under control, then speed up again."

- ✧ Missing estimates
- ✧ Customers won't make decisions
- ✧ Defect reports
- ✧ Not going end to end
- ✧ Failing daily builds
- ✧ Customer won't finish

Missing Estimates

If every time you come to the end of an iteration you have to throw away half of the stories, then something is definitely wrong. Iterations can have a moment of dramatic tension, but most iterations should finish comfortably. You might not know on the second Tuesday if you're going to make it, but when the lunch pizza comes on Friday and you push the button to run the acceptance tests, everyone should be confident of the outcome.

Are you committing to too much? Kent had a project where the programmers' guilt level was high enough that they always rounded up. "We got 38 days done last iteration with 4 people, so call that 10 days per person and we have a new person, so that's 50." They missed a little every iteration, but, more important, they got behind on testing and refactoring until finally one iteration completely pancaked. They delivered 1 (one) day to the customer. That was the wake-up call to just follow Yesterday's Weather.

Have you gotten behind on testing and refactoring? If so, you'll see debugging take an increasing percentage of time but an unpredictable percentage. The only solution we've found is to slow down, temporarily, and write the extra tests and do a little more refactoring. After a couple of iterations your speed should pick up.

Have you succumbed to the temptation to slice your estimates? It is so easy for programmers to feel guilty when the customer is disappointed and for that guilt to turn into shorter estimates, not for any technical reason, but because they want the customer to be happy (or at least stop bugging them). This doesn't work. Don't do that. When programmers make estimates, have them find comparable work and make the estimates comparably. "We have two new reports. They are both about the same as the framdoozle report we did last iteration, and that took a week. Call them a week each."

Customers Won't Make Decisions

Sometimes customers simply refuse to make decisions. They won't pick the stories for an iteration. They won't specify acceptance tests. They won't answer little questions about scope.

Extreme Programming cannot work without a customer making decisions. Customers don't have to stick with those decisions. Changing their mind is one of their rights. But the decisions must be made, and by someone with a business perspective.

Sam Gentile reports on a project where the customer's boss signed a contract for extreme development. When the team got there and started exploration the customer was incensed. "I hired you to do the analysis, not for me to do the analysis. Get to it. And I'm busy, so don't ask me any questions." Fortunately the team had the wisdom to terminate the contract at that point.

Find out why the customer won't make the decisions. If his priorities are elsewhere, perhaps the whole project doesn't make sense. If he doesn't want to be publicly wrong, the best you can do is reassure him that he will get a chance to fix any errors in the next iteration.

Defect Reports

Between the unit tests and the acceptance tests, the software produced by an extreme team should be remarkably defect free. There should be enhancement requests aplenty, but the software should work as specified.

If you are seeing enough defect reports to disrupt development, slow down until you aren't seeing them. Have a pair go through every defect and find where it occurred and what unit test should have been written to catch it, then report back to the team.

Sometimes a class of defects will turn into a design change. "We have six bugs when we run with Netscape. We have to create a browser object to isolate the browser-specific behavior."

Not Going End to End

It is so tempting to stop developing when you get uncomfortable. We're building a Web server and we've got all these tests, but they always run inside our network. Go out to Seattle Coffee, rent a station on the Internet, and try to get to the server. If we can't, because our proxy server isn't configured yadda yadda yadda, then stop until it is. Every dark corner you haven't explored with your flashlight is full of bugs.

Failing Builds

If the eight to ten integrations you do every day are going smoothly but you have problems when you push the software to production, make the integration environment match the production environment more closely. The feedback from the little integrations won't help your planning if you don't know how much progress you've actually made.

Customer Won't Finish

One of the failures we've seen in XP is where the customer flits from flower to flower—a few stories from here, a few from there. The programmers blaze along, hitting their estimates, finding fabulous abstractions while refactoring, testing like mad. Then one day the project is cancelled because it didn't get anything done.

Make three- to four-month release plans that the customer presents to upper management. Are the results of those plans reviewed when the date rolls around? The big cheeses are there for a purpose—use them. Big bosses can be good at spotting misfits at a quarterly scale, "I can see that all this Web stuff is exciting, but if we don't prepare for this Federal Reserve report we're out of business."

Chapter 27

Your Own Process

No two XP projects will ever act exactly alike. Once you get comfortable with the basic process, you will grow it to fit your situation more precisely.

We have been prescriptive here, telling you what to do to plan your software project. At the end of the day, however, you have to own your own plan and your own planning.

One way to adapt XP planning to your own situation is to take the bits and pieces of it that make sense and mix them with what you are doing now. The problem with mix-and-match is that the parts of XP planning are intended to complement each other. If the project manager estimates tasks then assigns them to programmers, the programmers won't have the same sense of ownership as if they did the task breakdown and estimates themselves.

Here's an alternative strategy. Adopt XP planning "by the book." Run for a couple of iterations. Then look at the problems you are having and experiment with each iteration.

- ✧ We aren't getting done on time. Let's try one-week iterations for a month.
- ✧ Let's have the customer check off the task boxes.
- ✧ Let's put targets for refactoring on a board.
- ✧ Let's start making our performance graphics visible.

Spend an hour or two each iteration reviewing past experiments and results and brainstorming new ones. If you have the ceremonial pushing of the acceptance test button at lunch on the last Friday of the iteration, you can spend the rest of the day talking about your process.

The shops where we've seen XP happily adopted are those where they have started simple and grown. Some of the variations seem pretty radical at first. But once the team explains the rationale for the new practices, they make sense.

The beauty of an iterative process with short iterations and lots of data is that you can perform many more experiments, and with much more precise measurements of the results, than would otherwise be possible. Take advantage of your data. Play with your process.

Index

Register Your Book

at www.aw.com/cseng/register

You may be eligible to receive:

- Advance notice of forthcoming editions of the book
- Related book recommendations
- Chapter excerpts and supplements of forthcoming titles
- Information about special contests and promotions throughout the year
- Notices and reminders about author appearances, tradeshows, and online chats with special guests

Contact us

If you are interested in writing a book or reviewing manuscripts prior to publication, please write to us at:

Editorial Department
Addison-Wesley Professional
75 Arlington Street, Suite 300
Boston, MA 02116 USA
Email: AWPro@aw.com

Addison-Wesley

Visit us on the Web: http://www.aw.com/cseng